EARTH
SONG

EARTH SONG

MICHAEL JACKSON
AND THE ART OF
COMPASSION

JOSEPH VOGEL

BlakeVision Books
New York

Earth Song: Michael Jackson and the Art of Compassion
Copyright © 2011, 2012, 2017 Joseph Vogel
All rights reserved.
Published by BlakeVision Books

www.joevogel.net

Cover photo courtesy of © Optimum Productions
By Jonathan Exley
Cover design by Anna Dorfman

Selections from *Dancing the Dream* courtesy of ©1992 The Estate of Michael Joseph Jackson.
Used by permission.

Lyrics to "Earth Song" courtesy of ©Mijac Music.
Used by permission.

All author interviews conducted by ©Joseph Vogel

Library of Congress Cataloging-in-Publication Data
Vogel, Joseph, 1981-
Earth Song: Michael Jackson and the Art of Compassion/ Joseph Vogel
p.   cm.

ISBN 13: 978-1976106477
ISBN 10: 1976106478
1. Jackson, Michael, 1958-2009—Criticism and Interpretation
2. Jackson, Michael, 1958-2009—Popular Music—United States—History and Criticism
3. Vogel, Joseph. I. Title.

1 2 3 4 5 6 7 8 9 10

Printed in the United States of America

Dedicated to Sofi and Jude

They that walked in darkness sang songs in the olden days—
Sorrow Songs—for they were weary at heart.
                                        – W.E.B. DuBois, 1903

Now, more than ever, the world needs leaders who can inspire their fellow citizens with a fiery sense of mission, not a nationalistic or military campaign but a universal crusade to save the planet. Unless mankind embraces that cause totally, and without delay, it may have no alternative to the bang of nuclear holocaust or the whimper of slow extinction.
                                        –*Time*, January 1989

A human being is part of the whole, called by us Universe, a part limited in time and space. He experiences himself, his thoughts and feelings as something separated from the rest—a kind of optical delusion of his consciousness. This delusion is a kind of prison for us, restricting us to our personal desires and to affection for a few persons nearest to us. Our task must be to free ourselves from this prison by widening our circle of compassion to embrace all living creatures and the whole of nature in its beauty.
                                        – Albert Einstein, 1950

CONTENTS

In the Beginning ♦ 5

Privilege and Pain ♦ 6

Man in the Mirror ♦ 8

We Are the World ♦ 11

If You Care Enough For the Living ♦ 15

Endangered Earth ♦ 15

I Feel Them Inside Me ♦ 23

This is Her Song ♦ 24

Sunrise ♦ 25

An Epic in Embryo ♦ 27

Heaven is Here ♦ 30

Let the Music Create Itself ♦ 32

Earth Trilogy ♦ 33

Make It Big ♦ 35

Discovering Everything You Can ♦ 37

HIStory in the Making ♦ 39

A Musical Apocalypse ♦ 41

Rise From the Slumberous Mass ♦ 46

Outsiders ♦ 48

Storytelling ♦ 50

Action ♦ 51

Reverse Apocalypse ♦ 54

Over the Top ♦ 58

The Body as Canvas ♦ 61

Legacy ♦ 63

An Adventure of Humanity ♦ 65

Performance Art ♦ 68

Epilogue ♦ 70

Facts ♦ 75

Timeline ♦ 77

Acknowledgments ♦ 79

Interview About Earth Song ♦ 81

Notes ♦ 89

EARTH SONG

In the Beginning

◆◆◆◆◆

Michael Jackson was alone in his hotel room, pacing.

He was on the second leg of his *Bad World Tour*, an unprecedented, 123-date concert spectacle that stretched over nearly two years. The tour would become the largest-grossing and most-attended concert series in history.

Just days earlier, Jackson had performed in Rome at Flaminio Stadium to an ecstatic sold-out crowd of over 30,000 fans. In his downtime, he visited the Sistine Chapel and St. Peter's Cathedral at the Vatican with manager Frank Dileo, Quincy Jones and legendary composer, Leonard Bernstein. Later, they drove to Florence where Jackson stood alone beneath Michelangelo's masterful sculpture, *David*, gazing up in awe.[1]

Now he was in Vienna, Austria, music capital of the Western world. It was here where Mozart's brilliant *Symphony No. 25* and haunting *Requiem* were composed, where Beethoven studied under Haydn and played his first symphony. And it was here, at the Vienna Marriott on June of 1988 where Michael Jackson's magnum opus, "Earth Song," was born.

The six-and-a-half-minute piece that materialized over the next seven years was unlike anything heard before in popular music. Social anthems and protest songs had long been part of the heritage of rock—but not like this. "Earth Song" was something more epic, dramatic, and primal. Its roots were deeper, its vision more panoramic. It was a lamentation torn from the pages of the Old Testament; a "sorrow song" in the tradition of slave spirituals; an apocalyptic prophecy with echoes of Blake, Yeats and Eliot. It conveyed musically what Picasso's masterful painting, *Guernica*, conveyed in art. Inside its swirling scenes of destruction and suffering were voices—crying, pleading, shouting to be heard. (*"What about us?"*)

"Earth Song" would become the most successful environmental song ever recorded, topping the charts in over fifteen countries and eventually selling over seven million copies. Yet critics never quite knew what to make of it. Its unusual fusion of opera, rock, gospel, and blues sounded like nothing on the radio. It defied almost every expectation of a traditional anthem. In place of nationalism, it envisioned a world without division or hierarchy. In place of religious evangelism or traditional humanism, it pleaded for a broader vision of ecological balance and harmony. In place of simplistic propaganda for a cause, it was a genuine artistic expression. In place of a jingly chorus that could be plastered on a T-shirt or billboard, it offered a wordless, universal cry.

Privilege and Pain

Jackson remembered the exact moment the melody came.

It was his second night in Vienna. Outside his hotel, beyond Ring Strasse Boulevard and the sprawling Stadtpark, he could see the majestically lit museums, cathedrals, and opera houses. It was a world of culture and privilege far removed from his boyhood home in Gary, Indiana. Jackson was staying in elegant conjoining suites lined with large windows and a breathtaking view. Yet for all the surrounding opulence, mentally and emotionally he was somewhere else.

It wasn't mere loneliness—though his prolonged isolation while on tour took its toll. It was something deeper—a pain that connected him to the pain of others, a pain indeed that he largely felt as he identified with the pain of others. As the author James Baldwin put it: "You think your pain and your heartbreak are unprecedented in the history of the world, but then you read. It was books that taught me that the things that tormented me most were the very things that connected me with all the people who were alive, or who had ever been alive."[2] So it was with Jackson. He described his childhood and adolescence as a time of profound sadness and isolation. Even at the height of his fame, during the *Thriller* years, he had mannequins put in his bedroom to make him feel less lonely. But books, music, movies, paintings—*art*—were his salvation. Art bound him to a larger world of struggle, suffering, magic and beauty. It gave his life purpose.

When a work of art moved him, he obsessed over it. He would cross into its creative space and dwell inside its emotions, its characters, its textures and stories — sometimes for hours, sometimes for days. One such obsession at this time was with renowned artist Gottfried Helnwein's *Beautiful Victims*, a series of hyper-realistic watercolors and photographs from the 1970s and 80s that depict children in states of anguish and solitude. Helnwein's work is rooted in German expressionism. His subjects are often bandaged and presented against stark backdrops, highlighting their wounded and alienated condition.[3]

Jackson eventually used two of these pieces in modified form for his *HIStory* booklet in 1995.[4] The photograph, "Lichtkind" (Child of Light), also served as inspiration for his song "Little Susie," which tells the macabre tale of a young girl who mysteriously dies after a life of neglect and abuse ("Lift her with care," he sings. "Oh, the blood in her hair").[5]

Jackson carried these images with him throughout his tour in 1988 until that July in Germany when he had the opportunity to meet the artist who created them. Jackson always felt a deep kinship with fellow artists—particularly those who somehow captured life the way he felt it. Gottfried Helnwein was surprised by how much Jackson knew about his work. He remembers the pop star asking very specific questions about his techniques and inspirations. Helnwein came away convinced that this was no mere superficial celebrity. "Not only do I think that he is highly intelligent but also outstandingly educated," he said of Jackson.[6] Helnwein did a brief photo shoot during his visit in which he focused on the singer's face with little lighting or makeup.[7] It was intended to capture the human being, not the icon, stripped down to his essence.

After their meeting, Jackson left a simple note to Helnwein that read:

Love to Gottfried Thanx for the magic
Michael Jackson[8]

Man in the Mirror

◆◆◆◆

Perhaps the most common trait associated with celebrity is narcissism. In 1988, Jackson certainly would have had reason to be self-absorbed. He was the most famous person on the planet. Everywhere he travelled, he created mass hysteria. The day after his sold-out concert at Prater Stadium in Vienna, an AP article ran, "130 Fans Faint at Jackson Concert."[9] If the Beatles were more popular than Jesus, as John Lennon once claimed, Jackson had the entire Holy Trinity beat.

Yet while Jackson enjoyed the attention—indeed, even thrived on it in certain ways—he also felt a profound responsibility to use his celebrity for more than fame and fortune. In 2000, *The Guinness Book of World Records* cited him as the most philanthropic pop star in history. Over his lifetime, he reportedly gave over $300 million dollars to charity, including to the Make-A-Wish Foundation, the Elizabeth Taylor AIDS Foundation, the NAACP, UNICEF, and the Red Cross, among dozens of others.[10] "When you have seen the things I have seen and travelled all over the world, you would not be honest to yourself and the world to [look away]," Jackson said.[11]

This indeed was the point of his hit song, "Man in the Mirror," which reached #1 on the Billboard Hot 100 in the spring of 1988. The song was about a personal awakening. It was about recognizing that change does not happen on its own. It requires that people become aware, that they care about more than themselves, and *do something*. "Who am I to be blind/ Pretending not to see their needs," Jackson sings. His performances of the song on the Bad World Tour were both the climactic finale of the show and its parting message. "Make that change," he summoned his audiences. In an era often characterized by individualism, greed, and materialism, it was an anthem of conscience and responsibility. Jackson donated all of the proceeds of the song to Camp Ronald McDonald for Good Times, which assisted children suffering from cancer.[12]

Even more significant than giving money, however, Jackson gave his time. At nearly every stop on his *Bad World Tour*, he visited orphanages and hospitals. Just days before arriving in Vienna, while in Rome, he stopped by the Bambin Gesu Children's Hospital, handing out gifts, taking pictures, and signing autographs. Before leaving, he pledged a donation of over $100,000 dollars. Before a concert in London at Wembley Stadium he visited Great Ormond Street Children's Hospital— the hospital to which author J.M. Barrie famously gifted the copyright, and royalties, for *Peter Pan*. Jackson spent hours talking to, holding, and comforting children at the hospital, some of who were terminally ill. According to a local news story, the pop star "sat some on his knee and told them stories"; he also "handed out dozens of presents, albums, photos, and T-shirts."[13] Jackson donated 100,000 pounds to the hospital. In addition, he left an undisclosed amount of money to the Wishing Well Fund to help the London's Hospital for Sick Children, which he also visited during his stay.

Throughout the Bad World Tour, before and after concerts, Jackson had under-privileged and sick children brought backstage. "Every night the kids would come in on stretchers, so sick they could hardly hold their heads up," recalls voice coach Seth Riggs. "Michael would kneel down at the stretchers and put his face right down beside theirs so that he could have his picture taken with them, and then give them a copy to remember the moment. I couldn't handle it. I'd be in the bathroom crying. The kids would perk right up in his presence. If it gave them a couple days' more energy, to Michael it was worth it."[14]

Everywhere the tour travelled, Jackson tried to give back in some way. In Detroit, he donated $125,000 to the city's Motown Museum; in New York City, he gave $600,000 to the United Negro College Fund; in Japan, he gave $20,000 to the family of a young boy who was murdered, and hundreds of thousands more to hospitals and schools. When the tour was over, he auctioned off his personal items, with all the proceeds going to UNESCO. This was the man whom British tabloids had taken to calling "Wacko Jacko," of whom *People* magazine, less than a year earlier, declared on the front cover: "He's back. He's bad. Is this guy weird or what?"[15] Jackson's kindness and compassion was not good copy; if it made the news at all, it was usually buried behind stories about his plastic surgery or pet chimpanzee.

We Are the World

◆◆◆◆

Jackson's philanthropy on the Bad World Tour was not new. In 1984, after his hair infamously caught fire while filming a Pepsi commercial, Jackson established the Michael Jackson Burn Center as part of the Brotman Medical Center in Culver City, one of only a handful of badly needed burn centers in the Los Angeles area. "I wanted to do something," he said, "because I was so moved by the other burn patients I met while I was in the hospital."[16] Jackson suffered excruciatingly painful second-degree burns on his scalp, but hospital staff remembers him spending much of his time visiting and comforting other patients. Jackson donated the entire amount he received from Pepsi for the accident—$1.5 million dollars—to the Burn Center. That year, Jackson also donated all of his performance money from the Victory Tour to charity—an estimated $5 million dollars.

In 1985, Jackson joined the U.S.A. for Africa effort, helmed by actor and activist Harry Belafonte and music manager Ken Krager. Inspired by the U.K. charity effort, Band Aid, and its musical vehicle, "Do They Know It's Christmas?" Belafonte's vision was to bring American artists together for an urgent cause: to raise money and awareness for a famine in Ethiopia that was leaving hundreds of thousands of people, including young children, starving and destitute. The famine was caused by a combination of factors: a complicated civil war, a corrupt government, and one of the most severe regional droughts on record. By 1985, an estimated one million people had died, according to the United Nations.[17] Belafonte reached out to producer Quincy Jones about putting together a song for U.S.A. for Africa. Jones, in turn, reached out to Lionel Richie, Stevie Wonder, and Michael Jackson. Since Stevie Wonder wasn't available, Jackson and Richie charged ahead.

Jackson's goal was to write a simple melody that anyone could hum, across cultures and nations, even if they didn't understand the lyrics. For "We are the World," he remembers going into dark spaces, a closet or a bathroom, and trying to imagine the people in Ethiopia: their lives, their suffering, their humanity. When he came up with some notes, he had younger sister Janet listen in. "What do you see when you hear this sound?" he asked her. "Dying children in Africa," she responded. "You're right," Jackson responded. "That's what I was dictating from my soul."[18]

Jackson continued to develop the song with Richie in the ensuing days and weeks. By early January, he had recorded a solo demo and sent it to Quincy Jones. Jones loved what he heard. "A great song lasts for eternity," the producer later reflected. "I guarantee you that if you travel anywhere on the planet today and start humming the first few bars of that tune, people will immediately know that song."[19]

The official recording session was scheduled for January 22, 1985 at A&M Recording Studio in Los Angeles. As Jones planned it, the stars would head over immediately after the American Music Awards, held that night at the Shrine Auditorium. He famously left a sign at the front of the building that read, "Check your egos at the door." The list of legends that filed in that night was remarkable: Ray Charles, Bob Dylan, Stevie Wonder, Diana Ross, Bruce Springsteen, Billy Joel, Steve Perry, Tina Turner, Cyndi Lauper, Willie Nelson, and Paul Simon, among dozens of others. "Here you had 46 of the biggest recording stars in the entire world in one room, to help people in a far-off place who were in desperate need," recalled Jones. "I don't think that night, that experience, will ever truly be duplicated again. I know and believe in the power of music to bring people together for the betterment of mankind, and there may be no better example of this than the collective that was 'We Are the World.'"[20]

Jackson skipped the American Music Awards that night and headed to the studio early to record his part. When the rest of the artists arrived, he, Lionel, Stevie, and Quincy helped them learn their individual parts and the chorus. He characterized the creation and recording process as a "spiritual" experience. Most of those in attendance agreed.[21] They describe a genuine sense of joy, unity, and purpose. "Every second of that night was magical," remembers Quincy Jones. "As artists, we are all just vessels for God's whispers, and I know God walked through the studio that night, a couple of times."[22] The final result, completed around 8:00 am, was a majestic, gospel-infused, seven-minute anthem that weaved the together the vocals of some of the greatest artists of the 20th century. The *New York Times* praised it as "more than an unprecedented communal collaboration among pop music's elite for a good cause—it is an artistic triumph that transcends its official nature."[23]

Some critics, of course, scoffed at the self-righteousness of the charity event—and the song. But Quincy Jones and Harry Belafonte were having none of it. "Anybody who wants to throw stones at something like this can get off his or her butt and get busy," said Jones of its critics. "Lord knows, there's plenty more to be done."[24] What impressed Belafonte most was simply the willingness of its participants to use their talents for an important cause. "Here you are with dozens of the best and most powerful artists in popular culture, who had relegated their managers to a place in Siberia — and as a consequence, it was completely art on art."[25]

"We are the World" was released that March and quickly became the fastest selling single in history, shifting just under a million copies in its first three days. It became the bestselling song of the 1980s, eventually selling over 20 million copies worldwide. More importantly, it helped generate proceeds of over $60 million dollars, which were used to send over 120 tons of supplies to Ethiopia, including high-protein biscuits, water, medicine, tents and clothing. Later funds were also used for over seventy recovery and development projects.[26]

Jackson was proud of what the song accomplished. The idea of thousands of malnourished children being fed because of a simple song thrilled and inspired him. It showed him in a very concrete way the power of music to bring people together, to raise awareness and action.

Yet he also realized it wasn't enough. "We Are the World" didn't end hunger or poverty; it didn't solve the complicated socio-political issues, power dynamics and institutional corruption that were largely to blame for the severity of the African famine. Critics were quick to point out these shortcomings, often deriding Jackson as "self-indulgent" and "naïve" for trying. Songs like "We Are the World" and "Man in the Mirror" were dismissed as simplistic, utopian sentimentality. Music critic Greil Marcus wrote off the former song as nothing more than a Pepsi jingle, while the *New York Times'* Jon Pareles dismissed the latter as "activism for hermits."[27] Jackson's social vision offered global idealism, triumph and easy resolution, they argued, while the material conditions of the real world only worsened.

It was a critique that haunted Jackson while he toured. He believed the critics had it wrong; he believed they couldn't *feel* what the music meant to people—what it meant to *him*. Change, he believed, began within individual hearts and minds. And that's where art reached people.

Yet he wasn't self-satisfied. In a 1987 interview with *Ebony/Jet*, Jackson was asked: "When you look in the mirror, are you happy with what you see?

"In what way?" he responded.

"Just when you look – in terms of that social philosophy?"

"I'm never totally satisfied," he said. "I always wish the world could be a better place. No, not at all."[28]

If You Care Enough for the Living

◆◆◆

While performing or helping children in face-to-face situations, Jackson could push away his feelings of inadequacy, doubt and despair. When crowds all over the world swayed and sang along to "Man in the Mirror"—when he could *experience* some small sliver of the world made harmonious—he was happy. He was in his element. But when he returned to his hotel room, the pain and confusion often returned.[29] "The contrast between the King of Pop on stage and the same person in private situations was enormous," remembers acclaimed Belgian composer François Glorieux, who first met Jackson in 1987 and went on to classically arrange several of Jackson's songs. "The press described him as an untouchable and impossible man. But I discovered a completely different guy: extremely sensitive, emotional and even shy...The first hour I met him he asked me to describe my childhood. He didn't interrupt me once and listened to the whole story of my youth when bombs destroyed my home and killed three members of my family."[30] Glorieux met with Jackson on two other occasions, in 1989 and 1990. He describes these meetings as "the most emotional of my musical career. It was fantastic to discover so many common points of view: passion for music (without limits); for peace and freedom; love for animals and nature; and last but not least, [a concern for] humanity."[31]

Publicist and author Howard Bloom, who worked with several legendary artists, including Prince and Billy Joel, describes Jackson "as the most remarkable person I've ever met in my life. No question about it... He had a capacity for wonder and awe beyond anything I've ever seen, beyond anybody else in my life. If you were looking at an artist's portfolio with him, he'd have the beginning of what seemed like an orgasmic experience, just opening the first square inch of a page... When you sat down to discuss a difficult issue like him cancelling his tour...it felt as if Michael's chest opened like golden gates and you could see 10,000 fans inside of him. His job was to champion those fans. He felt God had given him a gift."[32]

New Age author Deepak Chopra, who Jackson collaborated with on his second book, *Dancing the Dream*, had a similar impression of the elusive pop star. "When we first met, around 1988," he recalls, "I was struck by the combination of charisma and woundedness that surrounded Michael. He would be swarmed by crowds at an airport, perform an exhausting show for three hours, and then sit backstage afterward, as we did one night in Bucharest, drinking bottled water, glancing over some Sufi poetry as I walked into the room, and wanting to meditate."[33]

People sensed this sensitivity in Jackson from a very young age. Smokey Robinson called him an old soul in a little body. "In his heart, he carried other lifetimes," said Robinson, "It was more than having soul; it was soul that went deep into the soil of a whole people's history."[34] It was one of the qualities that made him such a compelling performer, even as a child. For all the joy and vitality he exuded, there was always a certain sadness, a world-weariness.

In his teens, Jackson began to develop the early seeds of his social vision and humanitarian ambition. "Politics can't save the world, so the music people should at least try," he said in a 1979 interview with *Blues & Soul*. "I could never just make records for people to buy and just get rich from. That's no good to me. There has to be more than that."[35]

Themes of brotherly love, acceptance, and social transformation populate his earliest self-written work. Perhaps the first real glimpse of the scale of what he hoped to achieve with his music came with the song and short film for "Can You Feel It." Written with his older brother Jackie, the song delivered a passionate message of racial unity "(the blood inside of you is inside of me") and global harmony (take the news to the marchin' men/ Who are killing their brothers/ When death won't do"). It was the sonic distillation of the peacock symbol that appeared on their previous album. "Throughout the ages," Jackson explained in the liner notes of the *Destiny* LP, "the peacock has been honored and praised for its attractive, illustrious beauty. Of all in the bird family, the peacock is the only bird that integrates all colors into one, and displays this radiance of fire only when in love. We, like the peacock, try to integrate all races into one through the love of music."

The short film for "Can You Feel It," a ground-breaking, ten-minute visual feast conceived and written by Jackson, explicitly incorporated the peacock symbolism. It also weaved in elements of sci-fi films like *2001: A Space Odyssey* and *Close Encounters of the Third Kind*, the language of biblical origin stories, and the sweep of astrophysicist Carl Sagan's *Cosmos* to communicate a message about cosmic love and interracial harmony.

Over the ensuing decade, Jackson grew and evolved, both artistically and intellectually. His education was largely self-guided, but he approached it with an insatiable curiosity. Everywhere he toured he studied the culture and the people; he visited museums, galleries and bookstores as well as hospitals and orphanages. He amassed a library of thousands of books, videos and tapes. He read widely, reached out to experts, and pursed issues that interested him passionately. Even his aversion to partisan politics dissipated somewhat by the late 1980s. While he was never a policy wonk, he began to see some of the motives, interests and forces that led to such widespread injustice, destruction and suffering.

In addition to the many charities he supported, his interest in global affairs ultimately led him to establish the Heal the World Foundation in 1992, based on the track from his *Dangerous* album. Jackson described that track as a "public awareness song" intended to raise money and consciousness for humanitarian issues around the world. The Heal the World Foundation was designed to be much more comprehensive than U.S.A. for Africa, addressing poverty, education, disease (including AIDS), and relief in the wake of wars, genocide and natural disasters.

The foundation was quite active in its first few years, dedicating funds and resources to inner-city youth, children's hospitals, and war refugees, among other causes.[36] "The only reason I am going on tour is to raise funds for [the Heal the World Foundation)," Jackson said at a press conference. "My goal is to gross $100 million by Christmas, 1993. I urge every corporation and individual who cares about this planet and the future of the children to help raise money for the 'Heal the World' charity."[37] In 1993, the *Los Angeles Times* reported that Jackson was pledging 1.25 million to inner-city Los Angeles children, many of whom were impacted by the Los Angeles Riots following the Rodney King verdict.

Jackson made his Heal the World Foundation the centerpiece of his iconic Super Bowl Halftime performance, transforming the typically hyper-masculine, nationalist, capitalist spectacle into a borderless utopian festival of love. "Today we stand together all around the world, joined in a common purpose," he told the massive crowd in attendance (and millions more watching at home), "to remake the planet to a heaven of joy and understanding and goodness. No one should have to suffer, especially our children. This time we must succeed." Jackson donated his $1 million performance fee to his Foundation.

Endangered Earth

◆◆◆

Before the idea came for "Heal the World," however, there was "Earth Song." The late 1980s proved to be a critical turning point—not only for Michael Jackson's social and political awareness, but also for the environmental crisis more generally. The news that year read like passages from ancient scripture: there were heat waves and droughts, massive wildfires and earthquakes, genocides and famine. Violence escalated in the Holy Land, as forests were ravaged in the Amazon, and garbage, oil and sewage swept up on shores. Meanwhile, there was growing evidence that the planet was getting hotter. In place of *Time's* Person of the Year, 1988's year-end cover story was dedicated to the "endangered earth." "This year," the magazine wrote, "the earth spoke, like God warning Noah of the deluge."[38] It suddenly occurred to many people that we were literally destroying our own home.

Of particular concern in the late 1980s was the rapid deforestation of the Amazon. Home to more than half of the planet's remaining rainforest land, the Amazon Rainforest is the most species-rich territory in the world. An estimated one-third of the planet's biodiversity is in the Amazon and one-fifth of its freshwater. Scientists estimate that the Amazon has between 85 billion and 100 billion tons of carbon stored in its trees and shrubs, which equates to about 11 years' worth of global emissions. It is also home to many indigenous communities whose way of life has frequently been threatened by deforestation.

In 1988 and 1989, international attention to the Amazon reached its height when projects such as the construction of a transoceanic highway, dams, and further clearing for large soybean ranchers threatened to destroy unprecedented amounts of rainforest. Several high-profile celebrities became involved, including actor Marlon Brando, Latin American author Gabriel García Márquez, and recording artist Sting.[39] Saving the rainforests became a rallying call for the socially conscious in the late 1980s. It was both an environmental issue and a human rights issue. Remarkably, the heightened public awareness and the collective efforts of many groups and individuals seemed to have a meaningful impact. By 1991, deforestation slowed to one of the lowest rates on record. By 1993, the unification of the Xingu indigenous lands gave birth to one of the most important rainforest reserves in the world (an estimated 6.7 million acres).[40]

The Amazon Rainforest, of course, was just one of many issues. 1989 was also the year of the infamous Exxon Valdez oil spill, which spewed 11 million gallons of crude oil into Alaska's Prince William Sound. People were horrified by the images of birds, seals, and fish covered in black oil. It was considered one of the most devastating human-caused environmental disasters in history. Months later the student-led protests at Tiananmen Square in China resulted in tragedy as over one thousand innocent civilians were massacred by troops with assault rifles and tanks. Numerous other environmental issues were receiving significant media coverage in the late 1980s: pollution, growing landfills, suburban sprawl, and early press regarding greenhouse gas effects and global warming. Meanwhile, still looming ominously in the backdrop was the ongoing threat of nuclear warfare.

In this context, the environmental movement was gaining unprecedented traction. While liberals were frustrated with President Reagan's reluctance to take bold action in his first term, environmentalism had yet to become as politically polarized as it would in the 2000s. Rather than entrench himself in opposition, Reagan eventually adapted and made some concessions. In 1984, he actually identified himself as an "environmentalist," a stance that would be near-blasphemous among modern-day Republicans. "Preservation of our environment is not a liberal or conservative challenge," he declared, "—it's common sense."[41] According to the environmental group, the Sierra Club, under pressure from grassroots campaigns and an increasingly environmentally conscious public, "more acreage was added to the National Wilderness Preservation System in the lower 48 states under Reagan than under any other president. Twenty-nine new wildlife refuges were established, encompassing a total of 500,000 acres; [and] 200 new plants and animals were added to the nation's list of endangered species."[42] Moreover, notes biographer Gil Troy, the president "signed, reauthorized, and often reinforced legislation, including the Clean Water Act, the Resources Conservation and Recovery Act, and the Superfund legislation."[43]

By the late 1980s, as George H.W. Bush took office, the environmental movement reached peak popularity. A Gallup poll released after the 1988 presidential election concluded that the environment was the No. 1 concern of the voting public. More surprisingly, the poll indicated that the United States could be capable of electing a president based solely on the candidate's environmental agenda by as early as 1992. In this political climate, George H.W. Bush, like Reagan, self-identified as an "environmentalist." Indeed, in campaign speeches and commercials he argued that he would be a stronger environmental president than his opponent, Massachusetts Democrat, Michael Dukakis.

In his first year in office, Bush put his promise into action, proposing massive revisions to the Clean Air Act to address acid rain, urban air pollution, and toxic air emissions. With Democrats in control of both the house and senate, the legislation easily passed in 1990. *The New York Times* described the legislation as Bush's greatest presidential achievement. "If it's true, as some say, that we're all borrowing the earth from future generations," said Bush in a speech that year at the President's Environmental Youth Awards, "it's also true that the earth will be preserved by millions of small decisions made every day by every one of us. And they're the kind of small decisions that make a world of difference, whether it's recycling aluminum cans, conserving water, turning off a light bulb, even just keeping the refrigerator door closed."[44]

As Bush's first term in office wore on, however, concerns about the environment took a backseat to the Gulf War (1990-1991), the Los Angeles Riots (1992) and a lagging economy. Unemployment continued to rise through the summer of 1992, and Americans suddenly cared less about global warming and greenhouse gases and more about finding jobs and paying bills.

In spite of the presence of then-Tennessee senator and environmental darling Al Gore as Bill Clinton's vice president, the waning enthusiasm about the environment continued in the Clinton era. Clinton was quick to acknowledge the threat of climate change, and environmental issues were part of his campaigns in both 1992 and 1996. In 1993, he released a 50-point plant to reduce emissions of greenhouse gases by 100 million tons. By the time he left office in 2000, however, levels were 15 percent higher than they were in 1990.

Clinton did have a relatively strong record on conservation, protecting over 58 million acres of forests. In 1997, he also signed the Kyoto Protocol, which committed the U.S. to specific greenhouse gas emission reductions; yet the treaty was never even submitted to congress, and therefore failed to be ratified and enforced. According to most political historians, Clinton's primary focus while in office was growing the economy. "Almost every policy measure that Clinton undertook," observes Paul Wapner, "had an eye toward economic growth, and economic productivity became the answer to all our woes. Clinton told us that growth would reduce welfare, crime, the federal deficit, and inadequate health care at home, and promote democracy, peace, cultural exchange, and individual liberty abroad. As Clinton pursued this vision through back-to-work welfare reform, fast-track trade talks, and market-opening policies across the globe, other social values had to translate themselves into economic productivity or fall by the wayside."[45]

By the time Michael Jackson released "Earth Song" in 1995, the context could not have been more different than when he started it. The environmental movement had lost momentum. The environmental organization, Greenpeace, went from 2.35 million members in 1990 to 350,000 in 1998.[46] But it want far beyond strictly environmental issues. Social idealists were becoming increasingly exasperated with centrist policies and inaction on issues concerning the environment, social justice, and human rights—so much so that Ralph Nader made his first run for president under the banner of the Green Party in 1996.

Meanwhile, apathy seemed to have settled in among the broader public. Young people in particular were disillusioned with politics, and skeptical that they—or anyone—could make a meaningful difference. A 1998 Stanford University study showed that malaise and cynicism was on the rise for all age groups, but most significantly among young people. Pop culture, whether shows like *Beavis and Butthead* and *The Real World*, or the lyrics of hip hop and grunge, reflected this. The default sensibility for mid-90s pop culture was alternately cynical, ironic, or nihilistic. It no longer seemed plausible in this context for popular art to speak to serious issues.[47]

I Feel Them Inside Me

Some people grow accustomed to reading or watching the news casually, passively. They become numb to the horrifying images and stories projected on the screen. Yet such stories frequently moved Jackson to tears. He internalized them and often felt physical pain in response. When people scoffed at his sensitivity or told him to simply enjoy his own good fortune, he got angry. He believed in the poet John Donne's dictum that "no man is an island." For Jackson, however, the idea extended to life in all forms: nature, animals, and people across countries, cultures and races (especially children)—the whole planet was connected and intrinsically valuable.

"[For the average person]," he explained, "he sees problems 'out there' to be solved. Maybe they will be, maybe they won't...But I don't feel that way—those problems aren't 'out there,' really. I feel them inside me. A child crying in Ethiopia, a seagull struggling pathetically in an oil spill...a teenage soldier trembling with terror when he hears the planes fly over: Aren't these happening in me when I see and hear about them?"[48] One time, during a dance rehearsal, Jackson had to stop because an image he saw earlier that day of a dolphin trapped in a net made him so emotionally distraught. "From the way its body was tangled in the lines," he explained, "you could read so much agony."[49]

When Jackson performed, he could feel these turbulent emotions surging through him. With his dancing and singing, he tried to transfuse the suffering—give it expression and meaning. It was liberating. For a brief moment, he could take his audience—and himself—to an alternative world of harmony and ecstasy. "There is no greater bliss," Jackson explained. "[You] become one with the music, one with the audience...You start to play off each other and start to know where you are going before you get there...You feel you are transformed."[50]

But inevitably, he had to come back down. The music would stop, the lights would dim, the crowd would file out. And he would be whisked away by his entourage to another hotel in another city.

This is Her Song

As was customary during the *Bad World Tour*, Jackson was smuggled into his Vienna hotel through the back staff entrance along with Bill Bray, his longtime security chief, and other members of his entourage.

Once inside, he typically showered off and read a book; sometimes he would sketch in his art pad or watch a movie. On the night after his concert at Prater Stadium thousands of fans converged outside the hotel, chanting his name. Jackson finally emerged in one of the windows, wearing a grey and blue pinstriped pajama top and red flannel pants. He waved below to the euphoric crowd before running back to the bathroom, signing some promotional photos and tossing them out the window.[51]

For however long his stay was in a given city, his hotel

room became both sanctuary and prison cell. The maids at the Vienna Marriott Hotel remember him being extremely private. When they came into clean or bring food, he "disappear[ed] into another room."[52] He was the biggest star in the world, but wanted nothing more, at times like these, than the anonymity of a normal person.

It was during this brief stay in Vienna, however, that inspiration struck. "It just suddenly dropped into my lap," he recalled of the moment.[53] Earth's song. A song from her perspective, her voice. A lamentation and a plea.

The chorus came to him first—a wordless cry. He grabbed his tape player and pressed record. *Aaaaaaaaah Oooooooooh.*

The chords were simple, but beautiful: A-flat minor to C-sharp triad; A-flat minor seventh to C-sharp triad; then modulating up, B-flat minor to E-flat triad.[54] *That's it!* Jackson thought. He then worked out the introduction and some of the verses. He imagined its scope in his head. Nobody could see what he saw yet. But they would.

This, he felt, would be the most important song he had ever composed.

Sunrise

The final date of the European leg of Jackson's Bad World Tour was in Liverpool, England. The location was no coincidence. Jackson saw it as a pilgrimage of sorts to one of the birthplaces of rock—the home of the Beatles. His visit incited a Beatles-like response. The massive Aintree Racecourse was secured to try to meet ticket demand. A ticket allotment of 125,000 sold out immediately. Meanwhile, hotels filled so quickly fans began camping outside the racecourse in the days leading up to the show. Traffic stretched for miles. The Liverpool police described the event as requiring the city's biggest planning and logistical efforts since the Pope visited in 1982.

Jackson stayed at the Atlantic Tower hotel in a suite with sweeping views of the River Mersey. His concert on September 11, 1988 included a brief tribute medley of Beatles songs and a stirring encore performance of "Man in the Mirror." As was the case on most of his stops, dozens of fans fainted. Jackson himself was about ready to faint from exhaustion by the end of the show. Performing was not just physically draining; it was also emotionally draining. He put everything into his shows. But he acknowledged to those close to him that he was worn out. He'd been on the road now for nearly four months and was eager to return home.

When he returned to the States, however, he didn't rest long before getting back to work. That tape he'd recorded in Vienna was still on his mind. On September 20, 1988, he laid down the first official demo of "Earth Song" in Westlake studio accompanied by Bill Bottrell on grand piano.[55] "What about sunrise/What about rain," he sings. His vocal is almost identical to what ended up on the record seven years later. The lyrics that followed those opening lines, however, were improvised and eventually changed. After the opening stanza, Jackson simply hummed out the parts. The main line of the chorus was there, but Jackson was still feeling out what to do with it. He laid down some harmonized ahhhhhs and oooohhs. While it was just a scratch vocal and piano, the foundational ingredients were in place: the intro, the chorus, even parts of the bridge and outro. It was the seed of something that would become much bigger.

An Epic in Embryo

Jackson's creative chemistry with Bill Bottrell was an important development in his career. A young, talented, but then mostly unknown engineer and producer, Bottrell (Jackson called him "Billy") began working with Jackson on the *Victory* album in 1984. He subsequently became a key member of the so-called "B-team" during the *Bad* sessions—a group of musicians and engineers Jackson liked to experiment with outside the purvey of Quincy Jones. While none of their collaborations made the *Bad* album, the pair developed a strong working relationship that would result in some of the *Dangerous* album's best tracks (including "Black or White" and "Give In To Me") and several other quality outtakes (including "Streetwalker" and "Monkey Business").

Bad was Jackson's last album with music legend Quincy Jones. The decision not to renew with Jones caused some frayed feelings, but Jackson felt the move was necessary for his artistic growth. The *Dangerous* album was his first chance to act as executive producer, and he was thrilled to finally be in complete creative control.

Bottrell was a surprisingly natural fit for "Earth Song." Prior to working with Jackson, his musical résumé was eclectic. He had found his way in the big leagues after being hired for an ELO project by renowned producer Jeff Lynne (who had also worked with the likes of Bob Dylan, George Harrison, Tom Petty and Brian Wilson) in the late 1970s. Throughout the 1980s, he continued to work with Lynne, while picking up freelance work as an engineer around Los Angeles. He was introduced to the Jacksons by John McClain, a talented executive in the urban music division at A&M Records who helped launch Janet Jackson's career in the mid-1980s (and later became co-executor of Jackson's estate along with the singer's long-time attorney John

Branca). His first time producing officially was on Tom Dolby's 1988 album, *Aliens Ate My Buick*.

Bottrell's musical roots were in blues, folk and country, but he could adapt to just about any style, from prog rock, to New Wave, to synth pop. In addition to his work behind the desk, he also played multiple instruments, including guitar, piano, drums and harmonica. By 1990 he had gone from obscure freelance engineer to the pinnacle of the pop music industry, working with icons like Jackson, George Harrison, and Madonna.

The success and commercial aspects of the industry, however, were uncomfortable for Bottrell. He loved music for the sake of music, not to satisfy corporate executives. Soon after his work on *Dangerous*, he fled the Los Angeles scene and built his own studio called Toad Hall in Pasadena. Here, he began working with "marginalized artists," emphasizing the qualities he valued in music: authenticity, spontaneity, and the rawness and immediacy of a live performance. Bottrell went on to produce the debut albums of Sheryl Crow and Shelby Lynne, both of which won Grammy Awards.

Jackson was drawn to Bottrell's more spontaneous, do-it-yourself sensibility, especially after a lifetime of working in the Motown ethos of perfection, and then with seasoned studio pros like Quincy Jones and Bruce Swedien.[56] It allowed him the freedom to experiment with different styles and approaches. Bottrell believed artists should tap into their musical roots, whatever those roots were. He created a loose environment in the studio, allowing Jackson to operate without the looming pressure of expectations. The first track they worked on together was the duet, "State of Shock," originally recorded with Freddie Mercury, and subsequently re-recorded with Mick Jagger. "I just did what I wanted to do [with the demo] in about twenty minutes while he stood there and watched, and I rocked it up really good...So I think Michael picked up on my openness to experimenting, and that wide-open/*what can this be* approach. You don't bring a lot of techniques or set goals, and that's what was fortuitous."[57]

Indeed, this approach resonated with Jackson. Over his

years working with Bottrell, he gradually gained more and more confidence in him. "Michael was always prepared to listen and put his trust in me, but he was also a sort of guide all the time," recalls Bottrell, "He knew why I was there and, among all the songs he was recording, what he needed from me...He has precise musical instincts. He has an entire record in his head and he tries to make people deliver it to him. Sometimes those people surprise him and augment what he hears, but really his job is to extract from musicians and producers and engineers what he hears when he wakes up in the morning."[58]

Like Matt Forger and others, Bill Bottrell sensed an intensification in Jackson's passion about social and ecological issues. It was a passion they shared.[59] They watched numerous documentaries together and discussed issues like deforestation, animal rights, and corporate exploitation. One day, Jackson brought in a VHS of the 1985 film *The Emerald Forest*, directed by John Boorman, which recounts the story of a Brazilian tribe (the "Invisible People") and rain forest under siege by corporate colonizers.[60] It is a familiar theme now—see blockbuster films like *Avatar*—but at the time of its release the movie was quite revolutionary, and drew public attention to the rapid destruction of the Amazon. Jackson loved the film and instructed Bottrell to watch and internalize it to "prepare" him to work on "Earth Song."[61]

When Jackson let Bottrell listen to his early draft of "Earth Song," the engineer was immediately taken by its two main melody lines. Both he and Jackson were excited about the potential of the song. But within days, the artist was off to Pittsburgh to resume the final stretch of the Bad Tour. For now, the song would have to wait.

Heaven is Here

◆◆◆◆

Several months later, after Jackson had returned and recuperated from the final leg of his tour, "Earth Song"—which was then referred to as "Earth" or "Planet Earth"—was one of the first songs he brought in to work on.

It was now the summer of 1989. He had recently moved to the Santa Ynez Valley, a hilly, picturesque area north of Santa Barbara. Longtime attorney John Branca, who had helped him secure the ATV/Beatles catalog in 1985, finalized the purchase of his new home in 1988. Jackson renamed the 2,700-acre estate Neverland Valley Ranch.

Neverland became his sanctuary and inspiration. He transformed its idyllic natural setting into a personalized paradise—populated with an artificial lake, trees, flowers, animals, tee pees, amusement rides, a movie theater, and even a Disney-like C. P. Huntington train. There were statues of children, frozen in their youthful vitality and bliss. Speakers throughout the property played music—most often whimsical classical pieces. Most importantly to Jackson, it was private.

Here, far away from the pressures and intrusions of Los Angeles, he felt a renewed sense of purpose and vision for his work. "Michael was inspired by touring and seeing the world," said recording engineer, Matt Forger. "He came back with certain impressions. His social commentary kicked up a notch or two. Most of the early songs we worked on—"Black or White," "They Don't Care About Us," "Heal the World," and "Earth Song"—were more socially conscious. His consciousness of the planet was much more in the forefront."[62]

Jackson's spiritual worldview had also transformed. Raised a Jehovah's Witness, he was taught to believe in a God that was rigid and demanding, including the commandment not to celebrate holidays or birthdays. The main purpose of life, he was taught, was to prepare oneself and others for Armageddon, which Witnesses believed was imminent and futile to try to delay or prevent. The goal of Witnesses was to become one of the elite righteous members—the 144,000— that would survive and preside over the earth once it was cleansed of wickedness. If one didn't make the top tier, they could still be part of a second class of Witnesses who were allowed to live in paradise.[63]

For much of his life, Jackson tried to believe these doctrines. He pored over the Bible and felt deep anxiety about his eternal salvation. He frequently asked questions of church elders about doctrines he found confusing or unfair. Yet by 1987, he had learned and experienced enough to decide to officially resign from the faith. In a poem, Jackson wrote, "But I have chosen to break and be free/ Cut those ties, so I can see/ Those bonds that imprisoned me in memories of pain/ Those judgments, interpretations that cluttered my brain."[64]

In its place, he developed a much more inclusive, liberating understanding of himself, the world and the divine, informed, in part, by his exposure to New Age, Eastern, and Transcendentalist ideas. "It's strange that God doesn't mind expressing Himself/ Herself in all the religions of the world, while people still cling to the notion that their way is the only right way," he wrote in his 1992 book, *Dancing the Dream*.[65] In another piece, in place of his prior conception of the afterlife, he writes: "Heaven is here/ Right now is the moment of eternity/ Don't fool yourself/ Reclaim your bliss."[66]

This new understanding had a profound impact on his creativity, including "Earth Song." If God wasn't a demanding father, but an inspiring presence or energy like music and nature—if the global destruction of Armageddon wasn't inevitable, as he was taught, but something to try to care for and heal—this had crucial implications for his artistic and social vision. It gave a new urgency to his work. It also helped push his social commentary into more direct, challenging territory. "Earth Song" wasn't about faith or triumph; it was about pain and indignation.

Jackson, of course, was still informed by his religious upbringing. "Earth Song" is rooted in the fervent jeremiads and apocalyptic passion of the Bible—but it was now liberated from one particular creed and fused with more social aims. Jackson wasn't content to simply wait for God to fix the world or placated by promises of paradise. As he later put it during preparations for *This Is It* in 2009: "It starts with us. It's *us*! Or it will never be done."[67]

Let the Music Create Itself

◆◆◆◆

By the time Jackson returned to Westlake Studio in June of 1989, he was bursting with creative ideas. On a board by the mixing desk, he put up a quote by John Lennon: "When the real music comes to me," it read, "the music of the spheres, the music that surpasseth understanding—that has nothing to do with me, 'cause I'm just the channel. The only joy for me is for it to be given to me, and to transcribe it like a medium... Those moments are what I live for."[68] The words resonated deeply for Jackson: "channeling" was exactly how he viewed creativity.

"Let the music create itself," he often reminded himself. To Jackson, Lennon was a kindred soul: a similarly eccentric talent with the ambition, idealism, and defiance to re-imagine the world.

Still, Jackson knew it took time and effort to achieve what he saw and heard in his head. Some songs could be completed within weeks, while others took months, even years. He sometimes compared the creative process to an artist chipping away at a sculpture. "[You're] just freeing it. It's already in there. It's already there."[69]

With "Earth Song," he had the foundation worked out, but he wasn't quite sure yet how to execute it. Like a director, he needed the right creative team to help realize his vision.

Earth Trilogy

Gradually, in the ensuing months, the various parts of the song began to take shape. "It became quite the obsession for both of us," recalled Bottrell.[70]

Jackson's early concern was getting its size and tone right. He wanted it to have the passion and soul of a gospel song, the momentum of rock, and the linear arc of an opera. He wanted a sonic landscape that borrowed from ambient and world music, yet still managed to be anthemic and accessible. He didn't want it to be too complex or abstract since the song was intended to move masses of people. The key, then, was to make it "feel simple," but layer it with detail, texture, nuance, and richness.[71]

Jackson originally conceived of "Earth Song" as a trilogy (similar to "Will You Be There"), comprised of a modern orchestral piece, the main song, and a spoken poem (later released by itself as "Planet Earth"). In total, it would have been approximately thirteen minutes long. The poem, a couplet with traces of Walt Whitman, was essentially a cosmic love song to the planet. "In my veins, I've felt the mystery," Jackson wrote.

>Of corridors of time, books of history
>Life songs of ages, throbbing in my blood
>Have danced the rhythm of the tide and flood
>Your misty clouds, your electric storm
>Were turbulent tempests in my own form
>I've licked the salt, the bitter, the sweet
>Of every encounter, of passion, of heat
>Your riotous color, your fragrance, your taste
>Have thrilled my senses beyond all haste

> In your beauty I've known the how
> Of timeless bliss, this moment of now.[72]

Jackson's sensuous language evokes a different kind of relationship with the natural world: one of intimacy, wonder, and respect. It rejects the traditional Western notion that humans "own" nature and can do with it as they please.

For Jackson, nature was a source of profound joy, inspiration, and rejuvenation. "The whole world abounds in magic," he wrote in a piece in his 1992 book, *Dancing the Dream*. "[Nature] has exposed the real illusion, our inability to be amazed by her wonders. Every time the sun rises, Nature is repeating one command, 'Behold!' Her magic is infinitely lavish, and all we have to do is appreciate it."[73]

Jackson worked with Jorge del Barrio on the orchestral introduction. An accomplished composer and conductor, del Barrio—who would later work with Jackson on several other songs, including "Who Is It" and "Morphine"— described working with Michael as "one of the most memorable experiences in [his] life." "He was so passionate about his music," he recalls. "We spent most of our time alone, creating. We were very much friends and creative forces together."[74] Jackson felt del Barrio was a perfect fit for what he hoped to accomplish with "Earth Song."

In contrast to the section of Beethoven's Ninth Symphony Jackson used to lead into "Will You Be There," the prelude to "Earth Song" was more ambient and primordial. It contained nature sounds, indigenous drums, deep synth pads, and lush strings. "I worked with Michael on creating an ominous sound," says del Barrio, "the beginning of the Earth as it might have sounded when it was created and life began and as it progressed into Mother Earth and eventually moved into 'Earth Song,' which tells of the demise of the planet in the hands of Man. Michael felt that this song was to be the one that ultimately would help save the world."[75]

According to recording engineer, Matt Forger, it was "very modern, very avant-garde. He wanted to change the rules of a pop song, to stretch and experiment. It was a completely different sound for Michael. The whole concept was very ambitious."[76]

Ultimately, however, Jackson couldn't quite get the tripartite concept to work together the way he had hoped and decided to simply stick with the main part of the song. Still, many of the early ideas and sounds were implemented in del Barrio's orchestral arrangement for the song, including the dramatic strings.

Jackson also brought in Toto band members, Steve Porcaro and David Paich, to assist with synth programming. The atmosphere of the track, he knew, was crucial. The listener had to really *feel* it for it to effectively transport them. It also had to have a "beginning, a middle, and an end."[77] It had to tell a simple story that could be understood across cultures and languages. The challenge was accomplishing all of this in six and a half minutes.

Make it Big

Jackson was looking for something particularly unique and powerful for the bass. He came across a sound he really liked in the work of Guy Pratt, a renowned guitarist who was playing bass with Pink Floyd at the time. Pratt had also recently played on Madonna's hit, "Like a Prayer" (which Bottrell engineered).

Through Bottrell, Jackson extended the invitation to work on the track, and Pratt accepted. After learning of Jackson's vision for the song and hearing a demo, he laid down a massive, experimental octave-pedal bass line at Westlake Studio.[78] The deep, soul-vibrating sound heard on the record was achieved by using an octave divider, so that the bass was playing in two octaves at once. "That's what gave it that grandiosity," explains Bottrell.[79]

Jackson loved it. Indeed, the effect was impressive to the most discerning professionals. "'Earth Song' has a deeper bass than any track I've ever heard," said Brad Buxer. "It's remarkable. Usually you can mix a song down to two tracks on half-inch analog and get a little more punch in the bass, but when you mix to digital you can't because it will distort. That track somehow holds more of the bass elements, it's more saturated—so it gives the illusion of more low-end than a CD can actually hold. Billy and Bruce [Swedien] were masters at that. There's a magic in shaping those low frequencies, pulling certain elements out so you can get other elements in. Psychologically, it makes the bass sound as big and rich as possible."[80]

Soon after Pratt's session work, legendary British drummer Steve Ferrone, best known for his work with Tom Petty and Eric Clapton, came in to lay down the drum parts. Jackson and Bottrell communicated how epic it needed to be, especially after the second verse.[81] "It's this very heroic rock rhythm," says Bottrell. "And the drums just explode. Michael kept saying, 'Make it big, make it big.'"[82] Jackson initially wanted electronic drums for the track, but Ferrone convinced him to give real drums a chance. "I said, 'I'll do a deal with you,'" recalls Ferrone. "I'll cut it with electronic drums if you let me have a go at it on real drums.' And he said okay."[83]

Jackson listened to the electronic drum part first and loved it. He didn't feel another track was even necessary. It was perfect. But Ferrone reminded him of their deal. "Alright," Jackson agreed with a smile.

A while later he returned to Westlake Studio, and Steve Ferrone and Bill Bottrell let him hear the live drum version. Jackson was over the moon. "The real drums just move the air off those speakers," recalls Ferrone. "He went from just sitting there, listening, to dancing around the room. And that's what they used."[84]

Once most of the elements were in place, the legendary Andraé Crouch Choir—who had previously sung on "Man in the Mirror" and participated on two other tracks on *Dangerous*—

came in the studio to sing their portion of the song's epic finale. The entire session was filmed (with multiple cameras) and reveals a remarkable scene of collaborative energy: Jackson and Bottrell getting sounds in place and discussing the arrangement; rehearsals and final adjustments being made to the set up and equipment; the choir gathering in a circle and delivering its majestic chants.

"We gave them a tape to rehearse to a few days before with Michael's lead vocal," recalled Bottrell, "and they came in with the most wonderful arrangement."[85] The grand stereophonic sound was captured using two Neumann M-49 microphones and a vintage EMT 250 for reverb. The result was a powerful, dramatic climax with the natural energy of a live exchange.

Discovering Everything You Can

Jackson and Bottrell continued to tinker with the track for over a year—the first several months at Westlake and later at Record One in Sherman Oaks, California. As the *Dangerous* sessions progressed, however, much of Jackson's attention shifted towards the rhythm tracks, particularly when new jack swing producer Teddy Riley was brought on board in early 1991. Still, Bottrell felt confident "Earth Song" would not only make the *Dangerous* album, but also serve as its centerpiece.

As the album was wrapping up in the fall of 1991, Bottrell submitted the stem tape, a simple multi-track that embodies the mix. The song was now titled "What About Us" and Bottrell considered it "finished" besides some final vocal overdubs. "It was one of our priority tracks from the beginning," he said. "I was very proud of it."[86]

Yet to his—and many others'—surprise, Jackson cut it from the final track list for *Dangerous*. Bottrell was deeply disappointed. "I wasn't present when they had the Sony people out to listen to all of the stuff at the playback, so I found out later."[87]

Jackson understood Bottrell's disappointment. He was disappointed as well. The song meant a great deal to him. Yet his ultimate commitment was to the song—it had to be just right before he could release it, and he didn't feel it was quite there.

All who worked with Jackson understood that he was a painstaking perfectionist: every detail, from conception to production to mixing and mastering, had to be exactly what he wanted before he would "lock it in cement." It could be frustrating at times. Some collaborators worked with him for months, and none of the resulting material ended up on an album. Sometimes he admittedly over-thought or overworked a track, when he should have simply stuck with an early version.

Yet frequently the perfectionism paid off, as some new revelation would occur to him that would make the song stronger. "Michael has always felt better really fleshing out something over a long period of time to discover everything that he can about it," acknowledged Bottrell. "There was a process that I learned well, that any MJ release went through: a process of vetting, re-thinking, replacing midi with live players, etc. It was a long process."[88] In many cases, the average listener probably wouldn't even notice the differences, but Jackson felt an intrinsic obligation to make his art "as perfect as humanly possible."

With "Earth Song," beyond the unfinished lyrics, his main concern was getting more momentum, energy, and power in the second half. While the falsetto cries (which Bottrell described as "very Marvin Gaye-ish") in the call and response were poignant, he wasn't sure it captured the outrage and urgency he wanted to convey. There were also some more minor nuances he wanted to tweak with the instrumentation and the mix. "Earth Song," then, would stay in the vaults for another four years as Jackson released, promoted, made music videos, and toured for the *Dangerous* album.

History in the Making

When recording began on the *HIStory* album in January of 1994 at The Hit Factory in New York, Jackson was excited to finally get back to work on "Earth Song." He felt confident it would find a home on the new record. The only questions were how to make it better and who to assist him in finalizing his vision.

As it turned out, Jackson was mostly satisfied with the demo he had worked out with Bottrell during the *Dangerous* sessions. The length, arrangement, and production remained almost exactly the same. Still, there were some crucial additions, most significantly in the climax of the song.

Jackson turned to renowned Canadian-born "hitmaker" David Foster to help finish the track.[89] The winner of sixteen Grammy awards, Foster had worked with legends like Chicago, Barbara Streisand, Whitney Houston and Celine Dion (he had also worked briefly with Jackson in 1978 during the *Off the Wall* sessions).[90] His specialty was the power ballad, though his work in this genre also gave him a reputation for affectation and hyperglossy production. In 1985, *Rolling Stone* described him as the "master of...bombastic kitsch."[91] In production style, he was almost the exact opposite of Bill Bottrell. Jackson, however, knew what he needed and what skills Foster brought to the table. For Jackson, the role of a producer wasn't to overtake the song; it was to help him achieve—at times in very specific detail—what he heard in his head. In the case of "Earth Song" he didn't need an overhaul, just small brush strokes.

Foster brought in talented orchestrator Bill Ross to give the track a fuller, more powerful sound, most notably in the surging brass parts.[92] "The orchestra added so much drama," said assistant engineer, Rob Hoffman. "It made this beautiful song into an epic."[93]

Another important addition was Michael Thompson, a highly regarded session guitarist. Before Thompson, David Foster offered the position to Eric Clapton, but either Clapton or Jackson (or both) passed on the idea. It is possible that Jackson remained concerned about Clapton's racist past.[94] Thompson, however—who had worked before with David Foster and Quincy Jones—ended up being perfect for the job. His bluesy phrasings echo Jackson's pained singing beautifully.

A new mix of "Earth Song" was completed at the Hit Factory in 1994.[95] Most of Jackson's engineers assumed at that point that the track was finished. Although Jackson was pleased with many of the improvements, however, he still wasn't completely satisfied.

When recording moved back to Record One in Los Angeles in the spring of 1995, Jackson and his team focused in on the final details. Matt Forger estimated that around 40 multi-track tapes were used in total. "It crossed formats. It started on 24-track, switched to digital. The detail and work that went into it was staggering."[96]

Jackson turned to sonic magician, Bruce Swedien, to re-record parts of his lead vocal. To capture the immediacy and intensity Jackson wanted, Swedien recorded with a Neumann M-49 tube mike (instead of his usual SM7) and had him get "as close as physically possible to the microphone, thereby eliminating almost all early reflections... I used no windscreen. I placed him as close as he could possibly get to this incredible old mike."[97] The results were subtle but palpable. "The real goal of music recording is to preserve the physical energy of the music and the musical statement itself," explains Swedien.[98]

Jackson saved the final ad libs for the last weekend of recording as he expected "to kill his voice" in the process. He told assistant engineers, Eddie Delena and Rob Hoffman, "I'm sorry, but I don't think any of us are going to sleep this weekend. There's a lot to get done, and we have to go to Bernie [Grundman for mastering] on Monday morning."[99]

Over the next few days, Jackson and a small crew of

engineers ate, slept, and breathed the music. "He stayed at the studio the entire time," recalled Hoffman, "singing and mixing. I got to spend a couple quiet moments with him during that time. We talked about John Lennon one night as he was gearing up to sing the last vocal of the record—the huge ad libs at the end of 'Earth Song.' I told him the story of John singing 'Twist and Shout' while being sick, and though most people think he was screaming for effect, it was actually his voice giving out. He loved it, and then went in to sing his heart out."[100]

As was his custom, Jackson sang that night with all the lights out.[101] From the control room, Bruce Swedien and his crew of assistant engineers couldn't see anything. Yet what they heard roaring out of the darkness was astonishing: it was as if Jackson was channeling from the lungs of the earth—a pained, fierce, prophetic voice, giving utterance to the suffering of the world.

Those who witnessed it could feel the hair standing up on the back of their necks.[102]

A Musical Apocalypse

The final version of "Earth Song" was a six-and-a-half minute tour de force that presented the human condition—and the condition of all life—in dramatic panorama.[103]

In the beginning is sound: the pulsing rhythm of crickets and birdsong, the vibrant cacophony of nature. It conjures a lush setting—perhaps a tropical rainforest—brimming with life and music. "I believe in its primordial form all of creation is sound and that it's not just random sound, that it's music," Jackson once explained.[104]

A cascading harp welcomes the listener in, conjuring a sort of edenic paradise. Two of Jackson's favorite composers, Debussy and Tchaikovsky, made frequent use of the harp to evoke dream-like worlds of wonder and enchantment. As a student of literature, Jackson was also no doubt well aware of the harp's rich symbolic import, particularly in the Bible and Romantic poetry, as an instrument of creative inspiration and divine communion.[105] Here, it seems not only to invite the listener into a sacred space; it represents the world at sunrise, as it awakes in all of its natural rhythms, patterns, and intricate beauty.

The sense of wonder in these opening seconds, however, quickly transforms into something more mysterious. A deep, primal sound encroaches, as the poet Wordsworth once put it, "like an unfathered vapour that enwraps, at once, some lonely traveller."[106] Then comes the piano hook, the chords capturing a mixture of melancholy and longing.[107] "What about sunrise, what about rain?" Jackson sings, "What about all the things that you said we were to gain?" His voice sounds world-weary, as he assesses what's been lost in the name of progress.

Sunrise and rain are symbols of natural renewal. In contrast, Jackson presents humanity's quest for short-sighted consumption, exploitation and "gain." "What have we done to the world?" he asks. "Look what we've done." Beneath his voice, a deep synth pad haunts the words like a shadow, the chords rising from the soil. His narration describes a world turned wasteland. "Did you ever stop to notice/ All the blood we shed before," Jackson sings, his voice quivering as it rises to falsetto, "Did you ever stop to notice/ This crying earth, these weeping shores."

With most singers such sentiments might come across as cloying or melodramatic.[108] Yet Jackson had a unique ability to inject words with weight—to make people feel them far beyond the way they look on a lyric sheet. As Marvin Gaye once put it: "Michael will never lose the quality that separates the merely sentimental from the truly heartfelt. It's rooted in the blues, and no matter what genre Michael is singing, that boy's got the blues."[109] In "Earth Song," Jackson is singing the blues on a cosmic scale.

With each verse, the music builds. The soulful guitar interjections refract Jackson's anguished sentiments. The majestic orchestration swells and subsides. The tambourine adds momentum to the chorus.

In the second verse, Jackson alludes to the peace that was "pledged" with "your only son" — a biblical allusion that shifts his queries from humanity to God (or perhaps addressing the two as one). When will these promises of peace and redemption be fulfilled, he is asking. Later, he also references the prophet Abraham and the "promised land" that was covenanted to his descendants. These are Job-like remonstrations to deity. "I cry unto thee, and thou dost not hear me," Job lamented,

> Did not I weep for him that was in trouble?
> Was not my soul grieved for the poor...
> And now my soul is poured out upon me;
> The days of affliction have taken hold upon me...
> My harp also is turned to mourning,
> And my organ into the voice of them that weep.[110]

Like an ancient poet-prophet, Jackson is "probing the limits of the Almighty," while posing profound questions on behalf of the wounded and abandoned.

At the heart of his lamentation is the age-old quandary of why the innocent must suffer ("Did you ever stop to notice/ All the children dead from war"). The tension of these unanswered entreaties builds through the verses before erupting into the pain-filled cries of the chorus.

Listen to the explosion of drums and earth-shaking bass after the second verse: this is the moment the song transforms from forlorn to righteous indignation. It is intended to rattle the complacent. The second chorus takes on more force and momentum, gathering energy like a storm. The power is amplified by the choir, which emerges as shards of sun from the clouds, piercing through the veil like the Heavenly host.

Before the song's climax, however, comes one last moment of reflection. Jackson's voice is fragile and vulnerable again, no longer the howling representative of the voiceless.

"Earth Song" is an excellent illustration of how versatile Jackson is vocally: it is a voice that "conjures the human in extremis"— extreme heights and depths, extreme vulnerability and power, despair and rage.[111] In the bridge alone, he moves from wonder-filled awe ("I used to dream/ I used to glance beyond the stars") to sudden panic and uncertainty ("Now I don't know where we are") to utter despair and outrage ("although I know/ *we've drifted far!*"). This bridge represents a threshold moment, a liminal state between what was, or could be, and what is.[112]

The epic climax that follows that pushes the song to new heights. The chorus cries unfold with greater and greater intensity. The air swirls with apocalyptic energy, "the tumult of mighty harmonies."[113] Jackson's voice is like Jeremiah ("the weeping prophet") in lamentation: "Are not all my words as fire...and a hammer that shatters rock?"[114] It is like Shelley's revolutionary call to the West Wind: "Drive my dead thoughts over the universe,/ Like wither'd leaves, to quicken a new birth...scatter[ed] as from an unextinguish'd hearth/ Ashes and sparks...The trumpet of a prophecy!"[115]

His call and response with the Andraé Crouch Choir unleashes voices that have been smothered. With each plight Jackson brings to our attention, the choir reinforces with the recurring chant, *What about us!*

> What about yesterday? *(What about us!)*
> What about the seas? *(What about us!)*
> The heavens are falling down *(What about us!)*
> I can't even breathe *(What about us!)*

The "us" is the amplified voice of the "Other": all who have been silenced, marginalized, oppressed or disregarded. Jackson is witnessing with them and allowing them to witness for themselves. It is a massive civil rights demonstration set to music.

The power of the exchange between Jackson and the choir is breathtaking. "What about the holy land?" he shouts, as the choir comes rushing behind like a torrent, (*"What about it!"*)

"Torn apart by creed *(What about us!)*/ What about the common man? *(What about us!)*/ Can't we set him free *(What about us!)*/ What about children dying? *(What about us!)*/ Can't you hear them cry? *(What about us!).*"

Then comes a slight deviation, as Jackson pleads: "*Where did we go wrong? Someone tell me why!*" His voice conveys desperation and bewilderment. How did we get here? How can it be accepted? *Someone tell me why!*

Finally, as Jackson reaches the end of his litany—exhausted, but unrelenting—he shouts, "*Do we give a damn?*" before letting out wordless exclamations of anguish. Language simply can't do justice to the pain and suffering he is trying to express and bring to the world's attention. In the background, the chorus cries continue as Jackson soars over the top.

The term "apocalypse" is typically understood to mean the destruction that will take place in the "end of days." Yet in the original Greek it means a "lifting of the veil," a revelation or prophecy that helps humanity to see what is hiding in plain sight.

"Earth Song," according to this definition, is a musical apocalypse. It takes the listener from an imagined paradise of harmony and vitality to our present state of degradation and divisions. Its final question ("*Do we give a damn?*") is about apathy. Why do we passively accept the way things are? Why can't we see and stop the self-destruction? Why can't we imagine and work toward something better?

Rise From the Slumberous Mass

◆◆◆◆◆

It is difficult to find parallels for "Earth Song" in popular music.[116] Bob Dylan's "A Hard Rain's a-Gonna Fall" offers a similarly prophetic, Biblically-rooted warning against self-destruction—released in the context of Cold War fears of nuclear annihilation—that both speaks to its time and transcends it.[117]

Other "protest songs," of course, have included environmental themes: Marvin Gaye's "Mercy Mercy Me," Joni Mitchell's "Big Yellow Taxi" and Neil Young's "Natural Beauty" and "After the Goldrush," among others.[118] But these tracks were much more modest and conventional in presentation, fitting rather neatly in the genres of folk or soul.

In terms of cultural impact, one parallel for "Earth Song" is John Lennon's classic, "Imagine." Both songs became global anthems with instantly identifiable piano hooks and choruses. Both ask listeners to try to care for the world we have, rather than simply be placated by the thought of an afterlife. Yet where "Imagine" makes a subdued, elegant statement, "Earth Song" is epic, intense, and visceral. This, indeed, is one reason "Imagine" is more palatable to the average music listener. Its radical ideas can be softened by its ethereal sound. "Earth Song," in contrast, seeks to shatter indifference, as it demands accountability. Radio can't do it justice. It is a song that was created to blast out of speakers if it couldn't be seen in person.

Stylistically, "Earth Song" combines elements of rock, opera, soul and gospel, but it is rooted in the sensibility of the blues. "He was the international emblem of the African American blues spiritual impulse that goes back through slavery," observes Dr. Cornel West. "Michael Jackson was part of that tremendous wave in the ocean of human expression."[119]

Indeed, the call and response form featured so prominently in "Earth Song" is a continuation of a long heritage in Black America that began with field hollers and spirituals.[120] "The core of gospel politics lies in the 'call and response' principle of African American culture," notes Craig Werner. "When the preacher or singer shapes a call, it is already a response to the shared suffering of the community. If the members of the congregation or audience recognize their own experiences in the call, they respond."[121]

In addition to giving voice to this "shared suffering," call and response has often been used as a form of resistance to oppression: by representing the voices of "the people" and their struggles, it allowed them to *perform* solidarity and gave them the strength to take action.[122] Nietzsche argued that it was in the bosom of this Primal Unity that human beings found deliverance and redemption.[123] One's suffering could be transfused into communal, creative energy. Jackson uses call and response, then, both to demonstrate our dire predicament as well as to showcase how we might collectively harness suffering for productive ends.

While "Earth Song" is clearly inspired by the Bible, Jackson revises the Judeo-Christian notion that nature is fallen and that men are given dominion over it. He draws from nature-oriented Eastern religions, including Hinduism, Sufism, and Taoism as well as Paganism and the indigenous traditions of Africans and Native Americans to introduce a sensibility of cooperation and harmony, not hierarchy and domination. "The Earth we share is not just a rock tossed through space, but a living, nurturing being," he wrote. "She cares for us. She deserves our care in return."[124]

"Earth Song" is also grounded in a rich tradition of prophetic poetry: William Blake ("O Earth O Earth return!...Rise from the slumberous mass")[125] and William Wordsworth ("I felt a sense of pain when I beheld/ The silent trees, and saw the intruding sky")[126]; W.B. Yeats ("The blood-dimmed tide is loosed, and everywhere/ The ceremony of innocence is drowned")[127] and W.E.B. DuBois ("Still quivering at unrighted Wrong;/ His soul aflame, and on his lips/ A tale of prophecy and waiting Work.")[128]

In terms of dramatic form, "Earth Song" is perhaps best understood in the tradition of tragedies. Like Greek and Shakespearean tragedies, it dramatizes the human struggle against fate. Yet Jackson presents this struggle, not from the perspective of royalty or heroic figures, but from the planet itself—from life as a collective (highlighting the voices of the wounded, vulnerable and invisible).[129] In "Earth Song," then, Jackson isn't merely representing himself. He is acting as the medium for a 21st century tragedy: the struggle of earth and its inhabitants for survival against increasingly overwhelming odds.

Outsiders

Jackson began preparing for the short film for "Earth Song" in the spring of 1995. The *HIStory* album had not yet been released, but Jackson was working overtime to ensure its success. His biggest priority was creating great music videos—he insisted on calling them short films—that continued to innovate and stretch the possibilities of the medium. That meant finding the right directors. For "Scream" he enlisted Mark Romanek; for "They Don't Care About Us" he brought in Spike Lee; and for "You Are Not Alone" he called up Wayne Isham.

For "Earth Song," however, he turned to a lesser-known name: Nick Brandt. Brandt is now best known as an acclaimed photographer, whose work features wild animals and nature primarily on the continent of Africa. In the early 1990s, though, he was an aspiring film director trying to establish himself through music videos.

Jackson first learned of the young British director after watching the music video for Whitney Houston's 1992 hit, "I Will Always Love You." Brandt's original cut of the video, as it turned out, was never seen by the public. "Clive Davis [then-

CEO of Arista Records] really did not like what I'd done," recalls Brandt, "and basically proceeded to completely annihilate the video, and render it a complete incoherent piece of shit."[130] Brandt was so upset with the changes he took his name off the video; it was replaced (as was common practice in those days when a video had no official director) with the fictional name, Alan Smithee.

Fortunately for Brandt, while most people thought he was crazy for pulling his name off of the Whitney Houston video, it ended up working in his favor, drawing more attention to his work. Ironically, Jackson chose to work with Brandt because he needed someone who could blend footage from a movie into a music video. His second single from *HIStory*, "Childhood," was being used as a theme song for *Free Willy 2: The Adventure Home*. After the director and Jackson met in person, however, they had other ideas.

In place of the *Free Willy* tie-in, which neither of them felt excited about, they began to conceptualize a Peter Pan-themed short. Jackson had long desired to play Peter Pan on screen, but that dream proved elusive after his planned collaboration with Steven Spielberg fell through for good in the early 90s. Brandt's treatment of "Childhood" was not a direct adaptation of *Peter Pan*, but it tapped into that whimsical world, portraying Jackson in a forest, with boats of children flying overhead. "I showed him all these storyboards," recalls Brandt, "we had these beautiful illustrated storyboards that were really lovely, to explain the concept to him."[131]

Jackson loved it. As with Bill Bottrell, there was a quick, natural rapport between him and Brandt. "Michael and I instantly got on because we were both kind of outsiders," explains Brandt, "We're both kind of prone to fantastical escapism, and obviously interested in the environment and nature."[132] They also both loved the art of storytelling. "I was always interested in doing videos that had a beginning middle and an end," says Brandt. "That told a story. I was really impatient with videos that you could basically chop out any particular sequence and it didn't really matter. With mine, ideally you would need to see it from beginning to end. It had a flow."[133] That philosophy, of course, was perfectly in sync with Jackson's philosophy. So much so, in fact, that the director would get the chance to work on two more of the *HIStory* album's most important songs: "Stranger in Moscow" and "Earth Song." The latter video came first.

Storytelling

In the early 1990s, Brandt was working for Propaganda Films, the biggest production company for music videos in the U.S. Propaganda boasted names like David Fincher, Michael Bay, Spike Jonze, Michael Romanek, and Dominic Sena. Jackson's first choice to direct "Earth Song" was an Indian director named Tarsem Singh (also represented by Propaganda), best known at the time for directing REM's music video for "Losing My Religion," which won Best Music Video of the Year at the 1991 MTV Video Music Awards. "Michael Jackson was obsessed with the video I did for Deep Forest [called 'Sweet Lullaby']," recalls Singh. "I was told, 'Michael wants you to hear this new song. Please come to LA and the song will be played for you.' I said, 'I have no interest in it.' Guess what? I loved the song. And I said, 'Okay, I'll meet him.'"[134] The collaboration fell through, however, according to Singh, because he refused to film Jackson's face.

Singh's loss was Brandt's gain. After working with Jackson on *Childhood*, Brandt was determined to convince the artist he was also the right person for "Earth Song." "I knew Michael had gone out to Tarsem for 'Earth Song,'" recalls Brandt, "and I was thinking, there's no fucking way I wasn't going to do that video. I was made to make that video. As it turns out, it's affected my whole life. I'm now doing what I do because of 'Earth Song.' That video changed the course of my life."[135]

Like Singh, Brandt was blown away by the song. He recalls listening to the playback of "Earth Song" in a studio and getting goose bumps. "I found it so moving, so powerful that it was pretty easy to write the idea for the script."[136]

Brandt took his cues directly from the narrative of the song. "That is the beauty of 'Earth Song,'" he explains. "It has a three-act structure."[137] For the video, likewise, Brandt presented Jackson with a concept in three acts: "You see the devastation, Act 1. Act 2, the people try to do something about it, and Act 3 is the earth healing itself."

To carry out this vision, Jackson needed a substantial budget. Sony refused to fund past $1 million, so, as the artist had done many other times throughout his career, Jackson put up his own money to achieve his creative vision. The video ended up costing $2.6 million, the second-most expensive video from the *HIStory* album, after "Scream"—and among the top twenty most expensive music videos made by any artist to that point. *Earth Song* was filmed on four continents: Europe, Africa, South America, and North America. It was scripted in May of 1995; pre-production began in June, and filming began in July, stretching over about six weeks into August.

Action

The original plan was to give the film a grainy, documentary-like feel, as if the events were unfolding in the news, but that plan was ultimately scrapped. There were many decisions, however, that gave the film a certain realism: the location shooting, the use of native people, rather than trained actors; even some of the camera movements, including the shaking effects and cross-cut editing with real-world destruction.[138]

As production commenced, the film presented numerous logistical challenges. Their first location, Karlovac, Croatia, was still a genuine war zone in 1995. "We couldn't walk down certain streets because there were still landmines," recalls Brandt "The villages were destroyed. No art direction was needed, because it was all real."[139]

In Brazil, where Jackson and Brandt hoped to draw attention to the destruction of the Amazon Rainforest, they looked everywhere for a timber company that would allow them to film trees being cut down, since they did not want to do it themselves. When they finally found one, they waited hours among suspicious crews with cameras ready to get the footage they needed. In Tanzania, where poaching was rampant, they had a life-size elephant mother and baby made out of fiber-glass to prevent harming any real elephants.

Brandt's only real frustration with Jackson had to do with lighting. As was the case for every video Brandt did with the artist, Jackson demanded that his face be highly illuminated, in part to hide self-perceived flaws and in part as an aesthetic preference. According to Brandt, the director of photography walked off the set multiple times in exasperation, but Jackson insisted. "The field we were shooting in was rendered fake by overlighting," said Brandt. "It wasn't designed to be lit that bright. Michael wanted so much light blasted on him I would literally have as many as 28 different mats running on his face, to reintroduce some semblance of shadow. We had to find some way to put shadow back in."[140]

Perhaps the biggest challenge, however, at all four locations, was producing the wind. In Kenya, they used Russian military helicopters as wind machines, which ended up blowing off the roofs of some Maasai tribe homes (Jackson paid for them to be re-roofed). In the Amazon, they used an airplane propeller with no grill. During one shoot, Brandt was talking to his art director, and forgot about the exposed propeller, which had gradually been inching towards him. An alert crew member jumped over and saved his life before he was decapitated.

Finally, in Warwick, New York, where they filmed the waste land scenes with Jackson, they brought in a 747 jet from across the country to serve as a wind machine. Unfortunately, all it ended up doing was producing a lot of noise and smoke, but not enough wind. "This was at three in the morning," recalls Brandt. "Can you imagine how the neighbors felt? This thing is roaring. I was so fucking embarrassed."[141]

They ended up using multiple large air movers from Home Depot, while members of the art department threw dust and twigs and leaves in the air. It was not easy on the artist, however. "Michael was getting hammered with this stuff," recalls Brandt. The debris was hitting him in the face, getting in his eyes. At one point, he pulled me aside, and said, "Nick, please, just one more take." We start rolling, and something went wrong, and I was screaming, 'Cut! Cut!', and nobody could hear me over the noise of the 747 jet, nobody could hear, and Michael just carried on singing and performing. He's getting hit with all of this debris. And at the end of it, I said, "Could you not hear me say, Cut!. " He just pulls out his earplugs, and says, "What?" The consummate professional, Jackson did another take.[142]

One of the most remarkable moments took place that night in New York. "I had a bunch of very cynical jaded New Yorkers for crew, for the part of the shoot that he was in. And they were just, 'Oh yeah, Michael Jackson, da-da-da-da-da...' But then when he started singing at the end of that song, and he's just screaming out the vocals....you could just see, you just look around and everybody had stopped in their tracks and watching him, riveted. And he'd only give me one take from each angle because he was getting blasted by these wind machines and stuff was flying in his eyes. I mean, it's really hard....And everybody was just electrified. He completely turned everybody around."[143]

Reverse Apocalypse

The final cut of *Earth Song*, the short film, was completed in the late summer of 1995. Like the song, it ran just under seven minutes, and like the song, it was organized in three acts.

It begins on the floor of the forest. The camera looks up, capturing the majesty of the trees, the diversity of animals. The sunlight sneaks through the branches and leaves. Rather than start with a distant establishing shot, the viewer begins inside, on the ground, an important choice. It offers an immediate sense of intimacy with nature, an intimacy that is quickly threatened when the camera stops at the sight of a bulldozer, plowing down the trees. It comes straight toward the screen, until the forest is gone. The screen turns black.

Suddenly we have jumped in time to a post-apocalyptic future. Here we see a solitary figure—Michael Jackson—dressed in tattered black and red clothes, wandering in a burnt down forest. The once vibrant forest has become a desolate wasteland. Around Jackson are tree stumps, ashes, and burning fires; the red-orange sky glows ominously in the distance. "What about sunrise," Jackson sings, "What about rain..." The film cuts to a medium shot. We see Jackson closer now. His sadness and fragility recalls a Steven Spielberg quote, in which he described the artist as "sort of like a fawn in a burning forest."[144]

After being introduce d to Jackson, the film cuts to a poached elephant, lifeless on the ground. It acts as a symbol for humanity's destruction of life in a barbaric, shortsighted exchange for wealth. Tanzania was once home to one of the largest elephant populations on the planet. Yet in the reckless chase for ivory, hundreds of thousands of elephants are slaughtered in the country every year. Sadly, that slaughter did not end in the 1990s.

Between 2009-2014, 85,181 elephants were killed in Tanzania alone. The camera dollies out to reveal indigenous Maasai tribespeople looking at the carnage; then zooms in to capture the pained emotion in their faces. Behind them, the land is bare and the sky is gray.

The film cuts back to Jackson in the burnt-down forest. This time, however, the camera tilts up and through the smoke we see the green forest again. Yet almost immediately, we see a tree being knocked down as native Amazonian Indians look on in dismay. The quick-cuts throughout this section of the video between Jackson in the burnt-down forest and these other groups of people and sites of destruction suggest a connection between them. What happens in Tanzania is connected to what happens in the Amazon Rainforest; what happens later in Croatia is connected to the wasteland in New York.

That suffering is embodied in the next shot, as Jackson holds out his arms and delivers the wordless chorus cry. The film cuts to a close up of a young black boy, his eyes filled with tears. Then to an elephant again, dead and mutilated; its baby lies next to it, also dead. As with the Amazon Rainforest, this scene of destruction briefly cuts backward in time, revealing a thriving ecosystem in which the elephants roam freely alongside various other animals. The quick cuts now are between Jackson and these beautiful animals: zebras, giraffes, and elephants.

Their stories, and lives, the films suggests, are connected too. The movement back and forth in time and space throughout the first half of the video is intended to not only highlight connections, but also contrasts and consequences: the world as it is, and the world as it might be (for better or worse).

The final location we see is Eastern Europe, in war-torn Croatia. Survivors walk among bombed buildings and ravaged streets, as soldiers rush by in the opposite direction. A tank rolls by. Often referred to as the Homeland War, Croatia's efforts to become independent came at a great cost: over 20,000 lives lost, 37 billion dollars in damage, and hundreds of thousands of displaced refugees.

The film cuts from Croatia back to Jackson in the wasteland; the blood-red sky looms behind him. He reaches out to touch a tree stump, and the film suddenly jumps back to the green forest, where Jackson's hand also reaches for a tree. Just as he is about to touch it, however, a chainsaw begins cutting it down; his hand flinches back.

The death of a tree in the Amazon cuts back to Croatia, where the people walk among wreckage and debris. We see a child's mangled bike; a family's surviving door frame. This was their home. A father looks at the bicycle and grimaces. The film jumps back in time again, where we see a beautiful green field. Children are playing; a young girl, perhaps the father's daughter, runs toward her bike. Once again, we see the contrast of what was, what could be, and what is. Like the homes in the Amazon and Tanzania, this home has also been destroyed.

The film cuts to Jackson again just as the song reaches its breaking point. The artist holds out his arms, then falls to his knees. He throws his head back, as if in agony. The Croatians also fall to their knees, as do the Tanzanians, and the Amazonians. Jackson digs his fists into the soil; the others do the same. They let it run through their fingers. They seem to be pleading with the earth to somehow not give up. "I had to come up with a device to try and show that the people who care about the destruction were trying to encourage the earth to fight back," recalls Brandt.

Then Jackson stops and looks up. "I used to dream," he sings, "I used to glance beyond the stars." His eyes convey a strange mixture of hope and betrayal. "Now I don't know where we are," he continues, shaking his head in dismay. "Although I know we've drifted far." Jackson's expressions here are devastating, and illustrate what made him so powerful on screen. The emotions he is able to capture—the sadness, loss and despair—are truly remarkable. This bridge is intercut with rapid-fire images of destruction: a factory belching out pollution; a dolphin trapped in a net; a seal being clubbed; a starving child in Africa.

The survivors, meanwhile, continue to kneel down in the dirt, massaging the soil and letting it fall through their fingers with zen-like focus. Suddenly the earth begins to shake, and the wind picks up. The pace of the video quickens; the cuts are rapid. Jackson looks up, as do the others; the wind is now rushing past like a hurricane; debris is flying all around them; lightning fills the sky; they look astonished, perhaps wondering if this is the end of the world.

Jackson stands up and raises his arms, embracing the chaotic energy; then pushed back by the wind, he grabs hold of two tree stumps. We see him first from the side; then in a medium shot, and finally in an eye-level close up. Then the camera moves underneath him, looking up; the low angle shot accentuates his strength and power amidst the surrounding storm, but it also allows us to see the sky above; a massive transformation is taking place; the earth itself is moving with velocity, as a mighty force or energy sweeps over it.

The survivors hold on for their lives, clinging to whatever they can, as they watch the earth gradually begin to heal itself.[145] Jackson stomps, and defiantly yells out his jeremiad; it is a call and response with the earth itself; the camera keeps shifting, moving, shaking, capturing the chaos and sheer force of the experience. The fallen trees rise again; tanks are pushed back; a dead Croatian comes back to life; pollution is sucked back into smokestacks; an elephant's tusks are restored.

Jackson delivers a series of punctuated cries. Animals run free again; they seem to be responding to the artist's exclamations. The rain forest is finally restored to its edenic state when the video began. It is whole again. The short film is, from one lens, Jackson's modern variation on the ancient myth of Paradise Lost and Paradise Regained.

Jackson's film, however, offers an interesting twist. The environmental apocalypse begins to reverse not through an act of God or even an act of science, but through the collective will of ordinary people, across borders. It reverses, that is—and this is what makes it such a unique iteration of the pastoral-apocalypse trope—by making connections.

Environmental change, he demonstrates, is not simply about saving the trees or the elephants; it is about how all forms of destruction are connected, as are all forms of life. It is about how deforestation is connected to poaching; it is about how the war in Croatia is connected to violence, imperialism and destruction elsewhere; it is about how nature is connected to the city, people to animals, and everyone and everything to the planet. "His grimaces are stark affectations of remorse, fear, anger and determination," observes film critic Armond White. "He's doing something almost miraculous—dramatizing hubris for the purpose of enlightening and improving life for others...His stance, holding on to tree limbs while buffeted by the winds of fate, is not sacrificial, it's not a crucifixion—it's a *positioning*. Michael is staking his beliefs in where and how we live."[146] It offers, that is, a radical intersectional vision. Only by understanding these connections and harnessing their power, the film suggests, can we hope to reverse course and heal.

Over the Top

The response to "Earth Song" from the entertainment media—both the song and video—was overwhelmingly negative, even hostile.

Released in November of 1995, reviews described it as "over the top," "bathetic," "cloying" and "sentimental." *Rolling Stone* wrote it off as a "showpiece...something with which to knock 'em dead in Monte Carlo."[147] Others scoffed about its concern for trees and whales and elephants.

Such assessments were perhaps more indicative of the critical and cultural sensibilities of the time than the song. Rock critics despised few things more in the 1990s than "sincerity." An earnest, socially conscious effort simply didn't have a chance in a decade dominated by cynicism, apathy, and irony. The days of social projects like U.S.A. for Africa, Live Aid and rainforest preservation were not only over, but remembered scornfully as celebrity vanity vehicles.

So averse was the United States in particular to the ethos of "Earth Song" that it wasn't even released as a single. Through much of the rest of the world, in spite of the criticism, it became a massive hit. It reached #1 in fifteen countries, one of Jackson's most successful global singles of his career. In the U.K., it became the artist's biggest single ever, selling over a million copies. In Germany, similarly, it became his bestselling single, staying at #1 for five weeks and attaining platinum certification.

Yet in the U.S., it was not released. This decision is even more noteworthy considering Jackson's previous single, "You Are Not Alone," was a #1 hit in the U.S. Yet for unexplained reasons, it wasn't offered to radio or record stores in America. Producer Bill Bottrell feels the decision wasn't by accident. "[The song] was anti-corporate, anti-nature-raping," he says. "So it was prone to censorship."[148] Even if it wasn't officially blocked, the fact that it wasn't seen as viable for U.S. listeners is telling.

The music video faced similar successes and similar obstacles. "When Earth Song came out, in those days it was a big deal," recalls Nick Brandt, "It was broadcast simultaneously on several TV channels around the world."[149] Yet it didn't take long before news stories began swirling that the making of the video was not environmentally sound—that trees had been deliberately chopped down and animals hurt. Jackson, they said, was just another celebrity hypocrite. "All this negative shit was going around," recalls Brandt. "That became the narrative. It was a distortion of something pure."[150]

A conference call was arranged by Jackson with his manager, Jim Morey, Sony head Tommy Mottola, and Nick Brandt. The artist was in tears. "Why does the press always have to distort everything?" he said. He wanted to arrange a press conference where he and Brandt could explain how the video was made and what it meant to him. His record company, however, said to leave the issue alone. "He was incredibly frustrated," recalls Brandt. "It was just lazy, corrupt journalism. Look at the bigger picture. Michael really, really cared. He couldn't have written that song had he not cared."[151]

Such defenses, however, didn't interest the critics. In simplest terms: Jackson wasn't cool anymore. For the media, he was more of a punch line, or punching bag, than an artist. His protest anthem didn't have the edge of hip hop or grunge. While those genres were often more insular, and in some cases, simply packaged myopic rebellion and nihilism, Jackson's big-picture plea was perceived as anachronistic, out of touch. The general public, particularly in a privileged country like the U.S., in the midst of an economic boom, preferred staring at its own reflection to looking outward.

The disdain for "Earth Song" also spoke to the general herd mentality in music journalism.[152] In this case, the knee-jerk consensus was that the song's theme, size and scope automatically equated to "pompous" and "bombastic." Few critics were able to actually consider the song on its own terms. No one, after all, would expect Queen to sound like Bob Dylan. "Earth Song" was big and dramatic because it was intended to be big and dramatic.

Yet it was clear that the biggest problem for critics was Michael Jackson himself. Since the mid-1980s, the media had developed a simple, but profitable portrait of Jackson that could be cut and pasted into each new story: He was a naïve, eccentric megalomaniac. Reviews of his music are almost universally interpreted through this lens beginning in the late 1980s, regardless of the merits of the song or album. Jackson, they often argued, should stick to the blissful "dance music" of his early career rather than some of the "angry," "defiant," "political" material that followed. Critics always preferred to view Jackson as an entertainer rather than an artist, a stereotype with a long racial history of which Jackson was well aware. As his music became more experimental and challenging, journalists tried in vain to put him "back in his place." They didn't want to hear songs about racism, media distortion, war and the environment from a pop star, they said. They wanted *Off the Wall* 2.0.

The Body as Canvas

Jackson's performances of "Earth Song" were likewise the subject of considerable controversy and criticism. Many critics interpreted them as the perfect illustration of Jackson's messiah complex. Jackson, they said, was pretending he had the power to magically solve all the world's problems. Did he really believe healing the planet was that simple?[153] Others were bothered by the visceral effect the performances had on crowds (audience members are often shown in concerts reaching out for Jackson and sobbing).

In the brief four years the song was performed (1995-1999), it served as the dramatic climax to Jackson's shows.[154] They were remarkable spectacles. Regardless of one's estimation of the song, watching him sing, stomp, howl, dangle precariously over the crowd, and pour out his soul on stage, at least made it clear why he was one of the most powerful artists of the modern era.[155] It was a potent blend of entertainment and art, prophecy and activism, music and visuals, carried out in a way that had never been done before.

The richness of these performances is only beginning to be properly contextualized and understood. "Jackson," writes acclaimed visual artist Constance Pierce,

> is often dramatically illuminated, while engulfed in a Baroque convolution of drapery, and raised high against the night sky on a 'cherry-picker' apparatus. Hovering above his massive audience, the illuminated drapery of

his silken cape unfurling, Jackson's mesmerizing presence gathers thousands below him into a participatory aesthetic, a 'performance art' ritual...Candles are lit and a torrent of arms lifts in unison. The gesture of passion embodied in Jackson's performance of 'Earth Song,' both iconic and transcendent, burns itself into the collective consciousness of the 20th century.[156]

This evocative description of the iconic, ritualistic, participatory nature of Jackson's performances gives a sense of what made them so transcendent and unifying for audiences.

Yet for all the pageantry and theatricality, it was the song itself and Jackson's ability to inject it with soul and passion that gave his performances such force. In perhaps his most stripped down rendition of the song at a one-off concert in Brunei in July of 1996, glistening with sweat at the conclusion of a three-hour show, Jackson delivers an impromptu coda (*"Tell me what about it!"*) that ranks among his finest moments on stage. There are no props, no pyrotechnics—just him, the mic, and the music.

The "messianic" charge gained more currency, however, after a performance at the 1996 BRIT Awards. In the middle of Jackson's biblically-inflected presentation, Pulp singer Jarvis Cocker stormed the stage and pulled his pants down to protest what he perceived as Jackson's "offensive" Christ-like imitation. Cocker was subsequently arrested and questioned by police about potentially injuring several child performers caught up in the incident. He was eventually released without charge.[157]

Jackson did indeed seem to be playing a messiah figure in the performance. What is strange is that so many people, including Jarvis Cocker, interpreted the performance so literally. Cocker was celebrated by journalists and some fellow alternative musicians (including Oasis) for his "brave" act (*Melody Maker* went so far as to say he should be "knighted"). Yet in retrospect it is Cocker's sanctimonious defense of Jesus that seems silly and egotistical. Jackson was using messianic gestures and symbols not because he literally thought he was the messiah, but because of what tapping into that archetype could express and communicate artistically. As a dancer and performance artist, his body acted as his canvas. "Embodying" the song meant becoming whatever the music and lyrics dictated to him. With this particular show, it was the best way he felt he could convey the song's agony, suffering and redemption.[158]

Legacy

Decades since it was first released, "Earth Song" remains overlooked by most critics.[159] While the great social anthems of Bob Dylan, John Lennon and Marvin Gaye are rightfully recognized among *Rolling Stone's* Top 5 songs of all time, Michael Jackson's "Earth Song" doesn't even crack the Top 500. Indeed, the song is rarely even acknowledged among *Jackson's* best songs.

Still, great art persists—and "Earth Song" has gained admirers over the years for its prescience and power. "I'm still very proud of it," reflects producer Bill Bottrell. "There is nothing else like it in terms of size and structure...It has the broadest scope, the most unusual blend of elements...It expresses such deeply felt, powerful emotions."[160] Director Nick Brandt, likewise, takes pride in the short film's emotional impact. "[Michael and I were] both interested in emotion which can become sentimentality or kitsch. But we wanted something deeper—there's a desire to move people and tell stories. I don't like sentimentality. If anything like that is there, I didn't do my job." For Brandt, it's greatest legacy resides in its message. "We're talking about something important: the survival of the planet," he reflects. "The fact that it's showcasing what we are doing to our planet—20 years on its only gotten a lot worse. A lot worse. As corny and cliche as it sounds, you're trying to make the planet a better place. There are different ways of doing it. No matter how small, it should not be dismissed. All of it counts. None of it should be dismissed."[161]

Indeed, in spite of the dismissals from contemporaneous media and critics, the short film for *Earth Song* was among the boldest to emerge from the 1990s— certainly one of very few music videos to grapple with serious, global issues.[162] Film critic Armond White praises the *Earth Song* video as being among "the most magnificent combinations of music and imagery in the centenary of motion pictures."[163] It won the Doris Day Award at the 10th Annual Genesis Awards from the Humane Society of the United States, as well as France's Le Film Fantastique: Best Video Award in 1996. It also received a Grammy nomination for Best Music Video, Short Form in 1997. It has been watched over 147 million times on YouTube.

Following Jackson's death in 2009, a resurgence of interest in the artist led many back to this unusual anthem and its haunting cry on behalf of the planet. It suddenly dawned on some people that long before terms like climate change, carbon emissions and "going green" became part of mainstream discourse, Michael Jackson was sounding the alarm, not only for the environment, but numerous other pressing social and political issues. In the 1990s, he was one of the most influential global messengers for environmentalism.

In recent years, "Earth Song" has been performed on popular shows like *American Idol*, *The X Factor*, and the Grammy Awards, among others. It has also been performed by symphonies around the world, from London to Japan. Globally, it continues to be one of his most beloved works.

Yet Jackson didn't just want the song to be sung or recognized. As he said in 2009, shortly before his death, he wanted the song to "open up people's consciousness."[164] He didn't want his audiences to simply feel bad; he wanted them to act. And that is precisely what many have done. Numerous educators now use "Earth Song" in classes to bring awareness to environmental, human rights, and animal rights issues. Green bloggers and organizers use it to draw interest to environmental activities and causes, particularly among young people. In 2010, a panel at the Schomburg Center for Research in Black Culture was dedicated to Jackson's song and its value and resonance to people of color.[165] Jackson's global fan base, meanwhile, is pushing to make "Earth Song" the official anthem of Earth Day.

"Earth Song" has also inspired activism. "After seeing the 'Earth Song' segment of *This Is It*," says Trisha Franklin, "I felt absolutely compelled to do something to help, as Michael asked. So I started a project to plant trees all over the world in Michael's name. 'A Million Trees For Michael' now has over 13,000 fans on Facebook and we get thousands of hits a month on our website. We have planted over 20,000 trees in the world and are hoping to plant thousands more."[166]

Such stories may seem insignificant given the scope and complexity of the problems confronting the world. But they are seeds. They represent resistance to a trajectory that Jackson recognized as not only unjust and unwise but unsustainable.

An Adventure of Humanity

Michael Jackson performed "Earth Song" to a live audience for the final time on June 27, 1999 in Munich, Germany.

The show was the second of two Jackson-organized benefit concerts (the first took place in Seoul, Korea) entitled "Michael Jackson & Friends – An Adventure of Humanity." All the proceeds—an estimated $3.3 million dollars—were donated to the Nelson Mandela Children's Fund, the Red Cross, UNESCO, and Kosovo refugees.

The day of the concert in Munich was scorching hot. Fans were given water to prevent dehydration.[167] In the early afternoon, the show got underway with performances by Luther Vandross, Ringo Starr, and Andrea Bocceli, among others.

As the sun faded and the air cooled, however, the anticipation began to build for Michael Jackson. Munich Olympic Stadium was now packed to the brim, a sea of humanity converged from all corners of the world.

Jackson hit the stage shortly after 11:00pm. As he stood motionless, *David*-like, amidst smoke and a flood of light, the excitement of the crowd was palpable. Jackson proceeded into a high-octane lineup of songs, including a deftly choreographed medley of "Dangerous" and "Smooth Criminal."

After finishing the set, Jackson ran back stage for a costume change and Gatorade while the elaborate backdrop was being built for his final number: "Earth Song."

During the break, Beethoven's "Ode to Joy" blared triumphantly through the warm summer air as lights surged through the crowd. Then, on the Jumbotron, a spinning globe appeared. The ecstatic mood suddenly turned contemplative as the moody, cosmic opening to "Earth Song" emanated through the stadium, followed by the mournful piano chords.

Jackson walks back onto the stage to the distant screams of fans, but mentally, one can tell, he is now inside his song.

He is dressed in black pants and a tattered black and red overshirt. His face is pale. He looks fragile and somber. "*What about sunrise...*" The unmistakable tenor sends a frisson through the crowd.

His gestures are expressive, dramatic, intended to communicate to the furthest audience member. On the screen, scenes of destruction are projected while Jackson stalks the stage restlessly.

As the song progresses, the tension gradually builds. Jackson's body crouches, pulses, and sways. He is channeling the painful emotions of the song. The chorus swells and releases like surging waves.

While Jackson sings, a huge steel bridge is erected on stage in three connecting parts. It was an addition to the number that had only been done once before, just a few days earlier in Seoul. The concept was intended as a sort of "Bridge of No Return": refugees are seen crossing over to what they can only hope will be safety and freedom. After they pass, Jackson runs up the bridge himself. Pyrotechnics explode on both sides, simulating the attack of jets dropping bombs from overhead. Guitarist, Slash, meanwhile, plays a tempestuous guitar solo below, heightening the sense of chaos.

Engulfed in a cloud of smoke, Jackson stomps and shouts, "*Someone tell me why!*"

Then the unexpected happens. After a series of explosions, the middle part of the bridge Jackson is standing on suddenly dislodges, rises, and then drops nearly sixty feet.

"From my angle, I couldn't see what happened, so I kept playing," recalls music director, Brad Buxer. "I could sense something was kind of strange, but I still heard Michael singing. When the smoke cleared, I saw the bridge had collapsed."[168]

Jackson's makeup artist, Karen Faye, said her "heart stopped beating" when she realized what happened. "Unlike rehearsals, and the last show [in Korea], [the bridge] didn't pause at its pinnacle," she remembers. "Instead it came careening down, gaining speed, with Michael tightly grasping the railings—still singing. I started screaming, but I could not even hear my own voice over the pyro, music, and the audience...From our vantage point we had lost sight of Michael...I could not imagine how [he] could have survived such a fall."[169]

The bridge landed with a thud in the orchestra pit in front of the stage.[170] Amazingly, while Jackson was shaken by the fall, he continued performing. The crowd in the front was stunned, but most of the audience simply assumed it was part of the show. Techs quickly jumped down to check on Jackson, but before they reached him, he was crawling back up onto the stage.

"I saw one arm reach for the floor of the stage," recalls Karen Faye, "then a long lean leg, another arm, another leg...He was up, center stage, finishing the end of 'Earth Song'! My mouth dropped open in relieved amazement."[171]

Concert organizer Briton Rikki Patrick later tried to offer an explanation for what happened. "We think a cable must have snapped or something. It was really frightening. People in the audience were screaming and crying. Security men were running everywhere. It must have been terrifying for Michael. But he managed to scramble back on stage. He staggered off to one side where I was standing and collapsed on to a chair. I could see he was in a lot of pain and bleeding at the back of his head."[172]

After the show, Jackson was rushed to Rechts Der Isar Hospital in Munich. He sustained a serious injury to his back and bruises. Yet before being whisked to the hospital, he insisted on not only finishing "Earth Song," but also the encore, "You Are Not Alone." The only thing he heard in his head, he later said, was his father's voice saying, "Michael, don't disappoint the audience!"[173]

After climbing back onto the stage from the dismantled bridge, surrounded by clouds of smoke, Jackson lets out his final exclamations. *Whoooo! Whoooo! Whoooo!*

Finally, with a single spotlight shining down, he stretches out his arms and looks out at the audience, drenched in sweat and depleted.

Performance Art

This might have been the end. Yet during the second leg of the *HIStory Tour* Jackson added a denouement. Just as the dust settles, a tank comes rumbling out onto the stage.

In the background, militant drums play over portentous strings. The tank is rolling toward the audience, but before it reaches them, Jackson jumps out in front, modeling the iconic imagery of Tiananmen Square. He is *performing* civil resistance— literally placing himself and his art against an imposing symbol of power and destruction. It beautifully emblemizes the meaning and purpose of "Earth Song."

A soldier then arises from the machine and points a gun at the refugees and Jackson. The audience gasps. He points it directly at Jackson's head as Jackson stares calmly back at him. The soldier has been trained to kill, but now, at the decisive moment he hesitates.

Unsettled, he nonetheless stands his ground, still aiming his gun at his unknown enemy. Then, from the side of the stage, a refugee child emerges. In tattered clothes, he walks toward the soldier carrying a flower. It is a symbol of life in all of its fragility, beauty and transience.

The soldier begins to come to his senses. He puts down his gun and takes off his helmet and goggles. As he looks into the boy's eyes, he drops to his knees and weeps.

The soldier and boy embrace, as do Jackson and the soldier. It is a scene of redemption and healing. In the background, the cascading piano notes fall like sheets of summer rain. The world may be filled with untold suffering and horror, yet here, Jackson demonstrates, is proof that there are still pockets of love, beauty, and music.

Flanked by the soldier, the child, and a group of refugees, he turns to his audience one final time, stretches out his arms, and tilts his head toward the sky.

Epilogue

◆◆◆◆◆

Michael Jackson expected "Earth Song" to be the most important piece of his *This Is It* concert series in London. He created an entirely updated concept for the number, including an introductory 3D film.[174] While he never saw it realized, his children introduced a tribute rendition at the 2010 Grammy Awards.[175] "Through all his songs, his message was simple: Love," said Jackson's oldest son, Prince. "Our father was always concerned about the planet and humanity ... We will continue to spread his message and help the world."[176]

On June 24, 2009, Jackson went through a rigorous three-hour dress rehearsal for *This Is It*. The elaborate show was almost ready to travel to London. His performance of "Earth Song" that night is painful to watch. He walks to center stage in black sweats, a black jacket, and red shirt and looks out at the mostly empty arena. Behind him, a large screen flashes the familiar imagery of a burnt-down forest. Jackson makes expressive gestures, almost like a form of sign language, as he sings; his face conveys unbearable sadness. When the chorus comes, he seems to collapse into it, waving his body and spinning inside its plaintive melody.

In the outro, he rides on the cherry picker, sparing his voice by singing in falsetto as he had on the earlier 1991 version of the song. He stomps and howls. Finally, the cherry picker brings him back to the ground. A bulldozer appears on the screen. In the actual show, Jackson planned for it to actually come out on the stage. He wanted the music to stop as the tractor door opened and a man emerged. "It's not the machines that are destroying the world," he wanted to convey, "it's the people that are destroying the world."[177] He insisted to director Kenny Ortega that the song not have a "happy ending." "I want it burning. I want it there, lasting and burning," he said, "and I want us standing there, with our arms reached out, asking people, 'please!'...before it becomes a travesty."[178]

In rehearsal footage from that night, Jackson is shown pointing out at his imagined audience, and saying: "You, you, you, us, we."[179]

"Earth Song" was the last song Jackson rehearsed before he died.

"I remember writing 'Earth Song' when I was in Austria, in a hotel, and I was feeling so much pain and so much suffering for the plight of the planet Earth. For me, this is Earth's Song, because I think nature is trying so hard to compensate for man's mismanagement of the Earth. And with the ecological imbalance going on, and a lot of the problems in the environment, I think Earth feels the pain, and she has wounds, and it's about some of the joys of the planet as well. But this is my chance to pretty much let people hear the voice of the planet. And this is 'Earth Song.' And that's what inspired it. And it just suddenly dropped into my lap when I was on tour in Austria."

—Michael Jackson, 1995

Earth Song Facts

RECORDED: 1988-1990, 1995 (Westlake Studio and Record One – Los Angeles); 1994-1995 (The Hit Factory – New York City)

CONTRIBUTORS: Written and Composed by Michael Jackson; Produced by Michael Jackson, Bill Bottrell, and David Foster; Lead Vocal by Michael Jackson; Choir: Andrae Crouch Singers Choir; Bass: Guy Pratt; Guitar: Michael Thompson; Piano: Bill Bottrell and David Paich; Tambourine: Bill Bottrell; Orchestration: Jorge del Barrio and Bill Ross; Synth Programming: Steve Porcaro and David Paich; Engineering: Bill Bottrell and Bruce Swedien; Assistant Engineers: Rob Hoffman and Eddie Delena; Mixing: Bernie Grundman

RELEASED: November 27, 1995

CHART PERFORMANCE: Australian Singles Chart (#15); Austrian Singles Chart (#2); Belgian Singles Chart (#1); Dutch Singles Chart (#1); Eurochart Hot 100 Singles (#4); Finnish Singles Chart (#1); French Singles Chart (#2); German Singles Chart (#1); Italian Singles Chart (#6); New Zealand Singles Chart (#4); Norwegian Singles Chart (#4); Spanish Singles Chart (#1); Swedish Singles Chart (#4); Swiss Singles Chart (#1); UK Singles Chart (#1)

RECORDS/ACHIEVEMENTS: Six weeks at #1 in the U.K. Five weeks at #1 in Germany. Certified platinum in the U.K. and Germany. In both countries it is Jackson's most successful single. Reached #1 on the Eurochart Hot 100 singles in 2009, nearly fifteen years after it was first released. Received a Genesis Award for animal sensitivity in 1995. Music video nominated for a Grammy Award (Best Music Video, Short Form) in 1997.

NOTABLE PERFORMANCES: Wetten Dass..? (November 4, 1995); Brit Awards (February 19, 1996); World Music Awards (May 8, 1996); Royal Brunei Concert (July 16, 1996); Seoul, South Korea Concert – Fan on the Cherry Picker (October 13, 1996); Munich, Germany Concert – Bridge Collapse (June 27, 1999)

SHORT FILM: Directed by Nick Brandt; Filmed at the Amazon Rainforest, Carlovac, Croatia, Tanzania, and Warwick, New York.

NOTABLE COVERS: London Symphony Orchestra; Mandolin Orchestra; Ne-Yo and Charice; Haley Reinhart; Melanie Amaro

ESTIMATED COPIES SOLD: 7 million

Earth Song Timeline

June 1988: Michael Jackson conceives of "Earth Song" in his hotel room in Vienna, Austria.

September 1988: Michael Jackson records the first demo of "Earth Song" with producer Bill Bottrell.

July 1989: Michael Jackson resumes work on "Earth Song" at Westlake Recording Studio D with producer Bill Bottrell.

October 1991: Michael Jackson decides to cut "Earth Song" from the final lineup of *Dangerous*, feeling it is not quite "ready."

January 1994: Michael officially begins work on the *HIStory* album, pulling Bottrell's stem tape out of the vault to re-work.

March 1995: Michael Jackson finishes the final ad libs for "Earth Song" and "locks it in cement."

November 1995: "Earth Song" is released worldwide as the third single from *HIStory*. By the end of the year it has reached #1 in over fifteen countries, but is not released as a single in the United States.

November 1995: Two days after the single is released, Michael Jackson performs "Earth Song" for the first time on the popular German TV Show "Wetten, dass..?"

December 1995: "Earth Song" stays at the top of the charts in Great Britain for six weeks, holding off the Beatles' first single in twenty-five years ("Free As a Bird"). "Earth Song" becomes his bestselling single in the U.K., selling an estimated 1.2 million copies.

February 1996: Michael Jackson performs "Earth Song" at the Brit Awards in London. The performance is marred by controversy when Pulp singer Jarvis Cocker storms the stage to protest Jackson's messianic symbolism.

June 1999: Eleven years after it was conceived, Michael Jackson performs "Earth Song" to a live audience for the final time in Munich, Germany. The performance is remembered for the bridge collapse that resulted in Jackson being rushed to the hospital.

June 2009: "Earth Song" is the final song Jackson rehearses at the Staples Center in Los Angeles, California. He is declared dead the next day, June 25, 2009.

Acknowledgments

I want to express my profound appreciation to Bill Bottrell, Michael Jackson's trusted friend, producer, and primary collaborator on "Earth Song." Your work with Michael will live as long as people listen to music. Thank you for the great conversations and fascinating stories about how this song came into being. Big thanks also to Nick Brandt, director of the majestic short film for "Earth Song," for our illuminating discussions about your experiences working with Michael. Thank you to Brad Sundberg for sharing the original "Earth Song" demo with me. Thanks also to Matt Forger, Bruce Swedien, Brad Buxer, Jorge del Barrio, and Rob Hoffman for your time, memories and insights about this song. This book wouldn't have been possible without each of you.

This book owes a great deal to Constance Pierce, for her artistic brilliance, wisdom, inspiration, and encouragement. It is also indebted to Armond White for being one of the few early critics to approach Jackson's work with the seriousness it deserves.

Thank you to Anna Dorfman for your generosity, artistry, and beautiful cover design. Thank you to Seven Bowie for your outstanding research and archives. Thank you to Manu Wedam for information about Michael's visit in Vienna. And thank you to John, Karen and the Michael Jackson Estate for your generous support and assistance.

I also want to offer my heartfelt thanks to the MJJ Justice Project team, the Michael Jackson Fan Club, MJ Vibe, Iconic Magazine, the Michael Jackson Tribute Portrait, the Michael Joseph Jackson Community, Fans United for MJ, Pay Michael Forward, Positively Michael, Michael Jackson Studies, and Dancing With the Elephant for your support of my work. A special thanks also to Spike Lee, Dr. Mark Anthony Neal, Dr. Michael Eric Dyson, Dr. Marie Plasse, Dr. Susan Fast, Dr. Willa Stillwater, Dr. Nina Fonoroff, Jenny Boyar, Mike Heyliger, Deborah Ffrench, Elizabeth Amisu, Karin Merx, Joie Collins, David Edwards, Chris Merante, Vera Serova, Damien Shields, Reverend Catherine Gross, Lauren Trainor, Tricia Franklin, Mary and Draven House, Bernard Zollicoffer, Bruce Aguilar, Sebastian Mille, and Pez Greaves for your valuable perspectives and contributions to Jackson's legacy. And finally, thank you to my family for your love and support.

APPENDIX

A Chat With Joe Vogel About Earth Song

From *Dancing With the Elephant: Conversations About Michael Jackson, His Art and Social Change.* Dr. Willa Stillwater and Joie Collins. September 29, 2011.

Joie: Willa and I are very happy to be joined by Joe Vogel this week. As you all know, his much-anticipated book *Man in the Music* will be released on November 1st, and now he's just about to release a print version of his ebook, *Earth Song.* Thank you for joining us, Joe! Here's what I would like to know first. Why did you choose to single out "Earth Song" and write a separate piece on it? Do you have a special affinity for the song yourself, or did you simply become intrigued by Michael's process – or obsession – with the song as you were researching for *Man in the Music*?

Joe: I've always loved "Earth Song." The power and majesty and passion of the song always just struck a deep chord with me. When I was working on *Man in the Music*, though, I was listening to all of Michael's work so closely that many songs made new impressions. "Earth Song" was one of them. The more I learned about it and the more I listened, the more convinced I became that this was Michael's most important song. It encompassed so much. The call and response with the choir, to me, is one of the most powerful moments I've ever heard in music. Yet there was so little recognition for the song among critics. Very little had been written about it that wasn't condescending and dismissive. So I wanted to somehow write about it in a way that would communicate its power – and I was excited about the prospect of really being able to zoom in on one song and do all the interviews and research with that kind of focus and depth.

Willa: I loved that! The level of detail you provide is wonderful, and I love the way your book provides insights both into "Earth Song" and into Michael Jackson's creative process as well. You begin your book by discussing how our world is in peril, and with descriptions of him experiencing that peril as an almost physical, wordless pain – and then you show him beginning to channel and shape and express those profound feelings into music. Can you tell us more about this process, and some key moments for how "Earth Song" came to be what we experience today?

Joe: Sure. I think, first of all, the process of "Earth Song" provides a great window into how Michael operated as an artist. That's what made it so much fun to write. You start making connections, putting pieces together. For example, I spoke with Matt Forger about this original concept of "Earth Song" as a trilogy (with an orchestral part, the song, and a spoken poem); after learning that, I returned to Bill Bottrell to figure out who the composer was that Michael was collaborating with and what it sounded like; Bill led me to Jorge del Barrio, who I subsequently learned worked with Michael on songs like "Who Is It" and "Morphine" as well. Through del Barrio I learned some wonderful insights about the concept and feel Michael was aiming for and how it transformed. So you speak to different people and all kinds of new connections emerge: new details, new angles. And you learn how carefully and thoughtfully Michael went about his work. In interviews, Michael tended to be really vague about his creative process, but what "Earth Song" reveals is how obsessed he was with every detail of his work from inception all the way to the final mix. He surrounded himself with great talent, but it was his creative vision and perfectionism that drove his projects.

Willa: You just highlighted something that really struck me when reading your book. You show that he was very knowledgeable and involved in the actual mechanics of creating "Earth Song" – that he was involved in every stage of the process. But in interviews he did tend to be vague about that, as you say, and kind of distanced himself from that aspect somewhat, focusing more on inspiration and being receptive to the song itself. He said in a number of interviews that the music just came to him and "fell in his lap." You write in your book that he often told himself to "Let the music create itself," and you tie this back to a quotation from John Lennon that he kept on display as a reminder to himself while working on "Earth Song":

> When the real music comes to me," it read, "the music of the spheres, the music that surpasseth understanding – that has nothing to do with me, 'cause I'm just the channel. The only joy for me is for it to be given to me, and to transcribe it like a medium.... Those moments are what I live for.

When I read this section of your book, I immediately thought of the Romantics. If we look at drafts of their poems, they did revise them and were in fact very knowledgeable and involved in the craft of creating poetry. They were skilled wordsmiths. But like Michael Jackson, they were reluctant to talk about that. They preferred to talk about creating poetry as an act of inspiration rather than craftsmanship, and tended to say they were merely scribes – writing down the words that some creative impulse larger than themselves expressed through them – rather than creators, which is an idea Michael Jackson frequently expressed. In fact, he kind of struggled to explain that during his deposition for the 1994 plagiarism case for "Dangerous," saying that he did write all of his songs, but in a way he didn't – they just came to him. I know you've studied the Romantics, so you know a lot more about this than I do. I was wondering if you could talk a bit about this Romantic ideal of the artist as merely a receptive channel for creativity to flow through, rather than a creator, and how that's reflected two centuries later in John Lennon and Michael Jackson.

Joe: A common metaphor in Romantic poetry is the Aeolian harp: When the wind blows, the music comes. You don't force it. You wait for it.

Willa: That's beautiful.

Joe: Michael believed strongly in that principle. But that being said, Michael was without question a craftsman. He rarely released work in raw form. Another metaphor he liked to use to illustrate his creative process is Michelangelo's philosophy that inside every piece of marble or stone is a "sleeping form." His job as an artist, then, was to chip away, sculpt, polish, until he "freed" what was latent. So it requires a great deal of work. You might have a vision of what it should look like, but you have to be in tune through-out the process and you have to work hard to realize it.

Willa: What a wonderful image! I love that idea of the "sleeping form," and it really clarifies how creativity requires both inspiration and craftsmanship. The idea of the song reveals itself to you and creates itself, as Michael Jackson liked to say; yet it requires the skill and dedication of a craftsman to free it.

Joie: Joe, in your book you talk about the absurdity of the fact that "Earth Song" was never released as a single in the U.S. even though Michael's previous U.S. single, "You Are Not Alone," debuted at number one. And yet, in other parts of the world, "Earth Song" was not only released as a single but went to number one in 15 countries. I agree with you when you say that decision was pretty telling – that the 'powers that be' didn't feel the land of excess would tolerate a song with such an 'in-your-face' look at the human condition. But, I believe that decision was a huge mistake. I think, had it been released here, it would have done very well. Despite the dismissive reviews it received, it is a difficult song to ignore and I think it would have gotten significant radio play if it had been offered to the stations.

Joe: You could be right. It's hard to know. On the one hand, Michael's popularity had waned in the U.S. because of the 1993 allegations. But his first two singles reached the Top 5. It's odd how quickly Sony seemed to bail on the album after that in terms of singles. It would have been nice to at least see the song given a chance with American audiences.

Joie: I love the way you compared "Earth Song" to John Lennon's "Imagine," saying that they both ask the listener to care for the world we have rather than dreaming of an afterlife. But can you talk a little bit about your statement that "Imagine" is more palatable to the average music listener than "Earth Song"?

Joe: Well, "Imagine" is an absolutely beautiful song that also happens to be quite subversive. Because it is so pleasant to listen to, and evokes such nostalgia, however, many people don't really catch on to the latter part. It calls for revolution, but plays amicably in dentist's offices and department stores. So some of its impact can be blunted in that way. When it plays at Times Square on New Year's Eve, it serves as a kind of feel-good anthem. There is nothing wrong with that. In fact, I think "Heal the World" is similar in terms of tone and psychological effect. But "Earth Song" is different. It has a different urgency and intensity to it. Imagine "Earth Song" blaring out of the speakers at full blast on New Year's. Better yet, imagine Michael performing it. Audiences would probably be stunned. The song wasn't designed to make people feel good; it was designed to prick people's consciences, to wake people up.

Joie: Which only makes me wonder all the more how it might have been received had it been given proper promotion and radio play in the U.S.

Willa: And if it didn't do well here, that would say something important too, since it did do well in many other countries.

Joe: Great, prophetic art is often neglected or misunderstood in its time. There are so many examples of this, from Blake to Van Gogh to Mozart to Picasso. Michael was a student of history and art and he understood this. He was confident that the work he created would hold up over time. "Earth Song" is a song that was, and continues to be, massively popular throughout the world. But ultimately it was a song that was going against the grain — so the resistance, from corporate executives, critics and other gatekeepers, makes sense.

"I respect the secrets and magic of nature. That's why it makes me so angry when I see these things that are happening in our world—I really, truly worry. Every second, I hear, the size of a football field is torn down in the Amazon. I mean, that kind of stuff really bothers me. That's why I write these kinds of songs, you know, to give some sense of awareness and awakening and hope to people. I love the planet. I love trees. I have this thing for trees—and the colors and the changing of leaves. *I love it!* And I respect those kinds of things. I really feel that nature is trying so hard to compensate for man's mismanagement of the planet. The planet is sick, like a fever. If we don't fix it now, it's at the point of no return. This is our last chance to fix this problem that we have. It's like a runaway train. And the time has come. *This is it.* People are always saying, 'Oh, *they'll* take care of it, the government will do it.' *They? They* who? It starts with us. It's *us*! Or it will never be done."

—Michael Jackson, June 2009

Notes

[1] This moment is shown in the documentary film, *Michael Jackson: Around the World* (1988). Jackson is dressed in black pants and a red shirt with his signature loafers and white socks. He walks toward the famous sculpture alone, in silhouette.

[2] *James Baldwin: Collected Essays*, Ed. by Toni Morrison (New York: Library of America, 1998).

[3] "My work is not an answer," says Helnwein. "It is a question."

[4] *HIStory: Past, Present and Future* CD Cover Booklet. Sony Music, 1995. p. 33: "Scream"- ("Das Lied/ The Song" watercolor, 1980); p. 37: "Little Susie"- ("Lichtkind/ Child of Light" photograph, grattage, 1972).

[5] Jackson shrugged off the criticism of such songs. "I don't care if people laugh or what they say. [Children] don't have a mouth to society...They need the world's awareness."

[6] Seven Bowie, "Beautiful Victim," MJJ-777.com, January 31, 2010.

[7] A portrait from this session now hangs in the Albertina Museum in Vienna, Austria. "He is extremely beautiful, fragile and totally unearthly," says Helnwein. "I always had the feeling that he is not standing on the floor but slightly floating on air. Michael Jackson knows that he appears like that on others and he also knows how to employ it."

[8] "Michael Jackson Meets With Helnwein in Germany." http://www.helnwein-music.com/article596.html

[9] "130 Fans Faint at Jackson Concert," *Associated Press*, June 4, 1988.

[10] Tina Daunt, "Michael Jackson's Generous Legacy," *Los Angeles Times*, July 8, 2009.
[11] *The Michael Jackson Tapes*. Shmuley Boteach. Vanguard Press, 2009.
[12] Tina Daunt, "Michael Jackson's Generous Legacy," *Los Angeles Times*, July 8, 2009.
[13] "In Ormond Street Hospital," http://www.truemichaeljackson.com/true-stories/in-ormond-street-hospital/
[14] J. Randy Taraborrelli, *Michael Jackson: The Magic and the Madness* (New York: Pan Books, 2004).
[15] The magazine was published on September 14, 1987.
[16] *Moonwalk* (New York: Doubleday, 1988), 238.
[17] "Flashback 1984: Portrait of a Famine," BBC News, April 6, 2000.
[18] *Moonwalk* (New York: Doubleday, 1988), 261.
[19] Billy Johnson, Jr., "Quincy Jones Recalls 'We are the World' Recording Session: 'Egos Were Checked at the Door,'" Yahoo, March 6, 2015.
[20] *Ibid*.
[21] See the documentary, *We Are the World: The Story Behind the Song*. Also, Robert Hilburn's article, "Behind the Scenes of a Pop Miracle," *Los Angeles Times*, March 24, 1985.
[22] Billy Johnson, Jr., "Quincy Jones Recalls 'We are the World' Recording Session: 'Egos Were Checked at the Door,'" Yahoo, March 6, 2015.
[23] Stephen Holden, "The Pop Life; Artists Join in Efforts for Famine Relief," *New York Times*, February 27, 1985.
[24] *Q: The Autobiography of Quincy Jones* (New York: Doubleday, 2001).
[25] "We Are the World Song Celebrates 20 Years," *Today*,

January 26, 2005.
[26] Jeff Wilson, "We Are the World Passes Goal," *Associated Press*, October 9, 1986.
[27] "Pop: Michael Jackson's 'Bad,' Follow-up to a Blockbuster, *New York Times*, August 31, 1987.
[28] *Ebony/Jet*, Interview with Michael Jackson, November 13, 1987.
https://www.youtube.com/watch?v=Dg6Xa8zadLQ
[29] "Any great artist is wrestling with their sadness and loneliness, their fears, anxieties and insecurities," observes Cornell West, "and they're transfiguring those into complicated forms of expression that affect our hearts, minds and souls and remind us of who we are as human beings, the fragility of our human status and the inevitability of death...[Michael] was able to express himself in such a way that he allowed us to have a sense of what it feels like to be alive." "Georgetown professor assesses Michael Jackson's cultural legacy." *The Tavis Smiley Show*. PBS. June 30, 2009.
[30] Seven Bowie, "François Glorieux: 'Do you know that he danced with me in his studio.'" MJJ-777.com. August 12, 2011. Also FrançoisGlorieux.com.
[31] *Ibid.*
[32] "The Truth: Howard Bloom Talks 2 Beautiful Nights," *The Beautiful Nights Blog*, October 26, 2014.
[33] Deepak Chopra, "A Tribute to My Friend," *Huffington Post*. June 26, 2009.
[34] Michael Jackson: Commemorative Edition. *Rolling Stone*. July 2009.
[35] Tamika Jones and John Abbey, "Michael Jackson's Peacock Music," *Blues & Soul*, August 28, 1979.
[36] While the intentions were noble, Jackson never had the

time or skillset necessary to sustain such a complicated operation over the long haul and the Foundation was reportedly disbanded in 2002.

[37] Dennis Hunt, "Jackson Plans World Tour To Fund Charity," *Los Angeles Times*, February 4, 1992.

[38] "Planet of the Year: What on Earth Are We Doing." *Time*. January 2, 1989.

[39] Beginning in late 1988, Sting teamed up with Chief Raoni (whose Kayapo people resided in the plain lands of the Mato Grosso and Pará in Brazil), embarking on a seventeen-country campaign to draw attention to the Amazon's plight. In 1989, he founded the Rainforest Foundation with his wife Trudie Styler, whose mission was to "to protect and support indigenous peoples and traditional forest populations in their efforts to protect their environment and fulfill their right to a secure, healthy and ecologically sound environment." Since 1989, it has helped protect over 28 million acres of forest and won several legal battles upholding the rights of indigenous peoples. It currently operates in over twenty countries.

[40] Unfortunately, by 1995—the year "Earth Song" was released—many people had lost interest and deforestation rates spiked higher than ever. Recent efforts to draw attention back to the Amazon Rainforest, and rainforests throughout the world, have made connections to climate change and shown their importance to sustainability.

[41] Gil Troy, *Morning in America: How Ronald Reagan Invented the 1980s*, (New Jersey: Princeton University Press, 2005), 143.

[42] *Ibid*.

[43] *Ibid*.

[44] Jim McGrath, *George Bush in His Own Words* (New

York: Scribner, 2001), 112.
[45] Paul Wapner, "Clinton's Environmental Legacy," *Tikkum*, March/April 2001.
[46] Kirkpatrick Sale, *The Green Revolution: The American Environmental Movement, 1962-1992* (New York: Hill and Wang, 1993).
[47] When Jackson started work on "Earth Song" in the late 1980s the zeitgeist was very different. Wrote Stephen Holden in 1987 for the *New York Times*: "Ever since "We Are the World," the all-star U.S.A. for Africa charity single and album two and a half years ago that launched a rash of charitable pop causes, there has been a movement within pop's higher artistic echelons to make music that addresses humane concerns." That movement continued for another few years before fading in the early 1990s.
[48] *Dancing the Dream: Poems and Reflections* (New York: Doubleday, 1992).
[49] *Ibid.*
[50] Shmuley Boteach, *The Michael Jackson Tapes* (New York: Vanguard Press, 2009).
[51] I was alerted to the existence of this footage by Michael Jackson researcher Chris Merante.
[52] Wiener Bezirkszeitung, "Wohnen Wie der King of Pop," Nr. 25, 23. Juni 2010. Translated by Manu Wedam.
[53] Jackson's full quote about how "Earth Song" first came to him: "I remember writing 'Earth Song' when I was in Austria, in a hotel, and I was feeling so much pain and so much suffering for the plight of the planet Earth. For me, this is Earth's Song, because I think nature is trying so hard to compensate for man's mismanagement of the Earth. And with the ecological imbalance going on, and a lot of the problems in the environment, I think Earth feels

the pain, and she has wounds, and it's about some of the joys of the planet as well. But this is my chance to pretty much let people hear the voice of the planet. And this is 'Earth Song.' And that's what inspired it. And it just suddenly dropped into my lap when I was on tour in Austria."

[54] Brad Buxer, a classically trained keyboardist who had worked with Stevie Wonder and was brought on board by Bill Bottrell that summer, was equally impressed. "The chorus is beautiful," he said. "I love stuff like that—triads to minor 7 chords. One of the most magical aspects of music is when you mix things up. A lot of basic rock and roll is triads, and jazz is complex chords. No jazz musician would say 'Earth Song' is tricky, but it's not about being complex. If it's done right, it's gorgeous. It's like poetry. Subtlety is everything. Michael had a beautiful sense of art." (Author Interview with Brad Buxer. May 16, 2011.)

[55] Huge thanks to recording engineer Brad Sundberg for making me aware of this demo and sharing it with me.

[56] "The main thing that I do as a producer, for better or for worse," says Bottrell, "is to orchestrate emotions in a room toward something...To get a good performance, you need to set a mood — a vibe — and this has to do with the people and the environment, the room they're in...I don't overly plan things. I like it loose, and I like it somewhat chaotic."

[57] Jake Brown, *Behind the Boards II: The Making of Rock n' Roll's Greatest Records Revealed* (New York Hal Leonard, 2014).

[58] Richard Buskin, "Classic Tracks: Michael Jackson's 'Black or White,'" *Sound on Sound*. August 2004.

[59] Bottrell became somewhat notorious in the music industry for his countercultural, anti-corporate, principled positions. This sensibility, however, was part of what made his role in "Earth Song" so important.
[60] Author Interview with Bill Bottrell. May 14, 2011.
[61] Author Interview with Bill Bottrell. May 14, 2011.
[62] Author Interview with Matt Forger. May 15, 2011.
[63] "Jehovah's Witness." *The Columbia Encyclopedia*. Columbia University Press. 2011. Also see James Penton's *Apocalypse Delayed: The Story of Jehovah's Witnesses* (Toronto: University of Toronto Press, 1997).
[64] *Dancing the Dream: Poems and Reflections* (New York: Doubleday, 1992).
[65] *Ibid.*
[66] *Ibid.*
[67] Michael Jackson's *This Is It*. Directed by Kenny Ortega. DVD. Sony Pictures, 2009.
[68] Matt Forger mentioned the John Lennon quote in one of our interviews, but couldn't remember exactly what it said. I subsequently found it in the background of a photo taken in the studio. The full quote can be found in the book: *John Lennon: In His Own Words*. Ken Lawrence. Andrews McMeel Publishing, 2005.
[69] Interview with Regina Jones, *Vibe*, March 2002.
[70] Author Interview with Bill Bottrell. May 27, 2011.
[71] "With Michael," explains Matt Forger, "the foundation may be deceptively simple, but so much is happening. So much detail and work. He understood contrast. He was very particular about texture. He wanted ['Earth Song'] to feel fresh and new and have this kind of epic weight and momentum." Author Interview with Matt Forger. May 15, 2011.

[72] *Dancing the Dream: Poems and Reflections* (New York: Doubleday, 1992).
[73] *Dancing the Dream: Poems and Reflections* (New York: Doubleday, 1992).
[74] Author Inteview with Jorge del Barrio. Translated by Ramon del Barrio. June 15, 2011. "Michael thought my father was extraordinary and they also spent a lot time laughing and making jokes," says Ramon del Barrio, after speaking to his father. "Dad and Michael worked together for many years and I am sure there are so many songs that were not released as well."
[75] Author Inteview with Jorge del Barrio. Translated by Ramon del Barrio. June 15, 2011.
[76] Author Interview with Matt Forger. May 15, 2011.
[77] While occasionally breaking his own rule, Jackson was a firm believer, in principle, in traditional forms of "storytelling."
[78] In interviews and comedy routines Guy Pratt tells a much more elaborate story about his experience. Jackson, he says, was hiding behind the mixing desk giving instructions through a Samoan bodyguard. While it's a funny story, I am told by reliable sources present during these sessions that it didn't really happen.
[79] Author Interview with Bill Bottrell. May 14, 2011.
[80] Author Interview with Brad Buxer. May 17, 2011.
[81] During the *HIStory* sessions, Bruce Swedien added a TC Electronics M5000, highly modified, "Wooden Hall" reverb on the drums to further accentuate their power. *In the Studio With Michael Jackson.* Hal Leonard, 2009.
[82] Author Interview with Bill Bottrell. May 14, 2011.
[83] "British Drum Icon – Steve Ferrone." *British Drum Icons.*

http://www.mikedolbear.co.uk/story.asp?storyID=1888.
[84] *Ibid.*
[85] Author Interview with Bill Bottrell. May 14, 2011.
[86] Author Interview with Bill Bottrell. May 27, 2011.
[87] Author Interview with Bill Bottrell. May 14, 2011.
[88] Richard Buskin, "Michael Jackson's 'Black or White,'" *Sound on Sound*. August 2004. Also, the Gearslutz forum, "Post here if you worked on Michael Jackson's Dangerous album," June 27, 2009.
[89] David Foster recalls of his time working with Jackson: "He was always engaged and focused, and my biggest complaint is that he had a tendency to do dozens of takes of every song. I can't think past eight takes, so it made me crazy. I'm not one of those genius chess masters who are always thinking seventeen moves ahead, so I found that part of it more than a little frustrating." *Hitman: Forty Years Making Music, Topping Charts & Winning Grammys*, David Foster (with Pablo F. Fenjves) Pocket Books, 2008. Foster also worked with Jackson on "Childhood" and "Smile."
[90] Foster co-wrote the song "It's the Falling in Love" with Carole Bayer Sager.
[91] Don Shewey, "Album Reviews: Kenny Loggins: *Vox Humana*," *Rolling Stone*. June 6, 1985.
[92] Says assistant engineer Rob Hoffman: "I've worked with Bill Ross on my own productions specifically because of the incredible arrangement he did on that song."
[93] Author Interview with Rob Hoffman. June 2, 2011.
[94] While Clapton deeply admired and borrowed from black musicians, including Robert Johnson, Jimi Hendrix and Bob Marley, he also notoriously spoke of the importance of keeping Britain white. In a 1976 concert in

Birmingham he said: "I used to be into dope, now I'm into racism. It's much heavier, man. Fucking wogs, man. Fucking Saudis taking over London. Bastard wogs. Britain is becoming overcrowded and Enoch will stop it and send them all back. The black wogs and coons and Arabs and fucking Jamaicans and fucking [indecipherable] don't belong here, we don't want them here. This is England. This is a white country. We don't want any black wogs and coons living here. We need to make clear to them they are not welcome. England is for white people, man. We are a white country." Clapton never apologized for these remarks.
[95] While still at the Hit Factory, Jackson wanted to re-record parts of his lead vocal on the track. The challenge, however, was matching his new vocals with the original ones. "We borrowed Bill [Bottrell's] U-47 mike and tried all of the Hit Factory's U-47's to see what matched, " recalls Rob Hoffman, "We eventually found one after a couple hours of listening." Later, they had to "fly in the EMT-250 reverb from the Hit Factory in New York, as it was used quite prominently in Bruce's original mix that he did in New York," recalls Rob Hoffman. "MJ wasn't satisfied with the Record One EMT's in this case. And he was right. We could all hear the difference." Author Interview with Rob Hoffman. May 24, 2011.
[96] Author Interview with Matt Forger. May 15, 2011.
[97] *In the Studio With Michael Jackson*. Bruce Swedien. Hal Leonard, 2009.
[98] *Ibid.*
[99] Rob Hoffman, "Post here if you worked on Michael Jackson's *Dangerous* album," Gearslutz Forum. June 27, 2009.

[100] "Later that night," says Hoffman, "while mixing, everyone left the room so MJ could turn it up. This was a common occurrence during the mixes, and I was left in the room with ear plugs, and hands over my ears, in case he needed something. This particular night, all the lights were out and we noticed some blue flashes intermittently lighting up the room during playback. After a few moments we could see that one of the speakers (custom quad augspuergers) was shooting blue flames. MJ liked this and proceeded to push all the faders up."
Rob Hoffman, "Post here if you worked on Michael Jackson's *Dangerous* album," Gearslutz Forum. June 27, 2009.
[101] "He always insisted on the lights being out," says Bruce Swedien. "The human being is primarily a visual animal. Light is distracting. Michael hated lights when recording." Author Interview with Bruce Swedien. May 19, 2011.
[102] "I've recorded just about everyone in music," says legendary recording engineer Bruce Swedien, who has also worked with Duke Ellington, Paul McCartney, Mick Jagger, and Barbara Streisand, among others, "and Michael is number one."
[103] "It meant so much to Michael," says Matt Forger. "It all came together in an incredible way. Everything was realized as completely as possible." It was a testament not only to Jackson's abilities as a composer and singer, but as an assembler and director of an eclectic team of musicians, producers and engineers. "What Billy brought to it was amazing, what David brought to it was amazing, what Bruce brought to it was amazing," says Brad Buxer. "But it was Michael guiding the whole thing—his perfectionism, his chords and lyrics, his execution."

[104] Robert E. Johnson, "Michael Jackson in Africa." *Ebony/Jet*. May 1992.

[105] In the Bible, the harp is often connected to David, King of Israel, composer of the Psalms, and probably the most renowned musician in the history of three major religions (Judaism, Christianity and Islam). In literature, the Aeolian harp—named after the ancient Greek god of the wind, Aeolus—symbolized the creative power of nature. When the wind blew, the music came. The Romantic poets frequently used the wind harp as a metaphor for the mysterious medium through which nature communed with the artist. The harp also represents spontaneity, wildness, and freedom. Its creative expression isn't calculated or premeditated. It isn't trying to be witty or ironic or important. It simply comes and is. Yet it also symbolizes transience. The music can leave as quickly and unexpectedly as it arrives.

[106] William Wordsworth, *The Prelude, Book VI*. 1805.

[107] The tone here is akin to what Wordsworth once captured in "Tintern Abbey" as the "still, sad music of humanity."

[108] Cover interpretations of the song tend to fall short not merely because of the difficulty of the vocal, but because of the depth and soul it requires.

[109] Michael Jackson: Commemorative Edition, *Rolling Stone*, July 2009.

[110] The Holy Bible, King James Version. Job 30. New York: Oxford Edition: 1769.

[111] Music critic Mark Greif used this description for the voice of Radiohead's Thom Yorke. "Radiohead, or the Philosophy of Pop," n + 1. Issue 3. January 2006.

[112] As Jackson put it in "Wanna Be Startin' Somethin'": "You're stuck in the middle/ And the pain is thunder."
[113] "Ode to the West Wind," Percy B. Shelley.1820.
[114] The Holy Bible, King James Version. Jeremiah 23:29. New York: Oxford Edition: 1769.
[115] "Ode to the West Wind." Percy B. Shelley.1820.
[116] I asked Bill Bottrell if he could think of any musical precedents for "Earth Song." His response: "Thematically, perhaps 'What's Goin' On.' Musically, it's probably most comparable to 'Man in the Mirror.' But there is more rock in it. 'Man in the Mirror' was more R&B fused with gospel. Also, I think "Earth Song," because Michael wrote it, was in some ways more personal, more internalized. You can feel it in his delivery."
[117] Most critics agree that Dylan's song is lyrically superior. Jackson's, however, is a more original piece of music and a far more dynamic vocal performance.
[118] Interestingly, Jackson's longtime musical rival Prince recorded a song nearly a decade later with very similar themes entitled "Planet Earth" (2007). Like Jackson's track, it combines scriptural allusions with green politics to epic effect.
[119] "Georgetown professor assesses Michael Jackson's cultural legacy." Cornel West. *The Tavis Smiley Show*. PBS. June 30, 2009.
[120] For context read W.E.B. Du Bois's chapter on the "sorrow songs" from *The Souls of Black Folk* (1900). Also, *Blues People* (1963) by Leroi Jones (Amiri Baraka).
[121] *A Change is Gonna Come: Music, Race and the Soul of America*. Craig Werner. University of Michigan Press, 2006.

[122] The communal dialogue in call and response is also a prominent feature in the choruses of Greek tragedies. In this context, it allows the community—and by extension the audience—to comment on the action of the "play" and thereby help construct its meaning. The chorus, in other words, invites the audience to participate in the unfolding drama.

[123] See Nietzsche's *The Birth of Tragedy*.

[124] "This we know," wrote Chief Seattle in an eloquent 1852 letter to the United States Government. "The earth does not belong to man, man belongs to the earth. All things are connected like the blood that unites us all. Man did not weave the web of life, he is merely a strand in it. Whatever he does to the web, he does to himself." *The Power of Myth*. Joseph Campbell (With Bill Moyers). Anchor Books, 1991. p. 43.

[125] "Introduction," *Songs of Experience*. William Blake. 1794

[126] "Michael," William Wordsworth. 1798.

[127] "The Second Coming," W.B. Yeats. 1920.

[128] "The Passing of Douglass," W.E.B. DuBois. 1900.

[129] "In his heart, he carried other lifetimes," said Smokey Robinson, "It was more than having soul; it was soul that went deep into the soil of a whole people's history." Michael Jackson: Commemorative Edition. *Rolling Stone*. July 2009.

[130] Author Interview with Nick Brandt. March 2, 2016.

[131] Author Interview with Nick Brandt. March 2, 2016.

[132] Author Interview with Nick Brandt. March 2, 2016.

[133] Author Interview with Nick Brandt. March 2, 2016.

[134] Craig Marks and Rob Tannenbaum, *I Want My MTV: The Uncensored Story About the Music Video Revolution*

(New York: Dutton, 2011).
[135] Author Interview with Nick Brandt. March 2, 2016.
[136] Author Interview with Nick Brandt. March 2, 2016.
[137] Author Interview with Nick Brandt. March 2, 2016.
[138] In retrospect, Brandt wishes they had shot the film in widescreen rather than the traditional 4:3 standard format. "It dates it," says Brandt. "It would have been incredible in widescreen."
[139] Author Interview with Nick Brandt. March 2, 2016.
[140] Author Interview with Nick Brandt. March 2, 2016.
[141] Author Interview with Nick Brandt. March 2, 2016.
[142] Author Interview with Nick Brandt. March 2, 2016.
[143] "Interview with Nick Brandt," all4michael.com, December 14, 2014. https://all4michael.com/2014/12/14/interview-mit-nick-brandt-regisseur-von-childhood-earth-song-stranger-in-moscow-cry-one-more-chance/
[144] Jay Cocks, "Why He's a Thriller," *Time*, March 19, 1984.
[145] "I was really proud of the editing in the final sequence," says Brandt. "I still get goosebumps watching it, when the earth is healing itself." Author Interview with Nick Brandt. March 2, 2016.
[146] *Keep Moving: The Michael Jackson Chronicles* (new York: Resistance Works). 76-79.
[147] "Michael Jackson's *HIStory*." James Hunter. *Rolling Stone*. August 1995.
[148] Author Interview with Bill Bottrell. May 14, 2011.
[149] Author Interview with Nick Brandt. March 2, 2016.
[150] Author Interview with Nick Brandt. March 2, 2016.
[151] Author Interview with Nick Brandt. March 2, 2016.

[152] As Anthony DeCurtis observes: "Much rock writing is snotty, adolescent, and dismissive...Rock critics have routinely aspired to supplanting their subjects, and they've succeeded at least in their own work and their own minds, if nowhere else." Anthony DeCurtis. Foreword. *Reading Rock and Roll*, Ed. Kevin H. Dettmar. Columbia University Press, 1999.

[153] Brandt takes issue with this literalist interpretation. "One of the things I'm very keen to clear up is what was going on in the final section of Earth Song. This is important to me. I came up with an idea in which at the end everybody was clinging for dear life to whatever they could, that was near at hand, while this almighty, apocalyptic, planetary wind blasted across the surface of the planet. Everyone just had to hold on, and now just wait while the earth healed itself. Now Michael, being the extraordinary, magnetic, charismatic, glorious performer that he was—and also singing the best part of the song—when he gets blown back and grabs hold of those two trees, that was never meant to be some Jesus crucifixion thing. It was never meant to be that he is bringing the earth back to life on his own. But because of the sheer power of his performance in comparison with non-professionals -- those are genuine Amazonian Indians, those are real Croatians, those were Maasai tribe people—they didn't have this extraordinary charisma and ability to perform like Michael did—so it got knocked out of balance. If you were predisposed to feel prejudicial toward Michael Jackson as an egomaniac, you ended up looking at that video and saying, "Oh, for fuck sake. He's doing this whole messianic, Jesus Christ thing, where he's trying to save the world." But that was not the intention at all. Perhaps I was

being naive. But it was supposed to be about us, "What about us," as he sings, and what we must do *together*." While Jackson is at the center of the film, then, it was not Brandt's intent to portray him as a "messiah," but rather as "the voice of one crying in the wilderness." Author Interview with Nick Brandt. March 2, 2016.

[154] Jackson also rehearsed the song in preparation for his *This Is It* concert series at the O2 Arena in London. However, he never had the opportunity to perform it to a live audience again after 1999.

[155] In a performance at Olympic Stadium in Seoul, Korea on October 13, 1996, a young male Korean fan somehow managed to elude security and climb up onto the cherry picker as it hovered high over the audience during the climax of "Earth Song." Jackson seemed shocked at first, but alertly grabbed hold of the fan to prevent him from falling. For the remainder of the song, Jackson clutches the fan tightly as he continues singing. When the cherry picker came back down to the stage, the fan was torn away by several security guards. The performance can be seen on YouTube.

[156] "Lacrymae Rerum: Reflections of a Visual Artist Informed and Inspired By Gestures of Transcendence in the Passionate Art of Michael Joseph Jackson." *Passions of the Skies in Fine Arts Expression*. International Society of Phenomenology. Fine Arts and Aesthetics 16th Annual Conference. Harvard University. May 18, 2011.

[157] In a statement, Cocker said that his "actions were a form of protest at the way Michael Jackson sees himself as some Christ-like figure with the power of healing." Jackson released his own statement through Epic Records, which

read: "Michael Jackson respects Pulp as artists but is totally shocked by their behavior and utterly fails to understand their complete lack of respect for fellow artists and performers. His main concern is for the people that worked for him and the fact that children should be attacked. He feels sickened, saddened, shocked, upset, cheated, angry but is immensely proud that the cast remained professional and the show went on despite the disgusting and cowardly behavior of the two characters that tried to disrupt it."

[158] "When Jackson embodies a particular archetypal stance," notes Constance Pierce, "his physical body transfigures into a kind of symbolic, elegant calligraphy wherein the Divine may channel gestures of explosive emotion or intimate compassion. The artist becomes shamanic, taking on our massive cumulative 'shadow' and sweeping it whole into the light. "Lacrymae Rerum: Reflections of a Visual Artist Informed and Inspired By Gestures of Transcendence in the Passionate Art of Michael Joseph Jackson." *Passions of the Skies in Fine Arts Expression*. International Society of Phenomenology. Fine Arts and Aesthetics 16th Annual Conference. Harvard University. May 18, 2011.

[159] Since Jackson's death in 2009 it *has* received some attention from academics, including essays by Willa Stillwater, Constance Pierce, Marie Plasse, and Gerd Buschmann. Such in-depth analyses from a variety of academic fields will allow "Earth Song" to be contextualized and interpreted in ways critics failed to do upon its release. (Gerd Buschmann's essay was published in German. "Der Sturm Gottes zur Neuschöpfung:

Biblische Symboldidaktik in Michael Jacksons Mega-Video-Hit Earth Song. Katechetische Blätter. Vol. 121, no. 3, pp.187-196. 1996.)

[160] Author Interview with Nick Brandt. March 2, 2016.

[161] Author Interview with Nick Brandt. March 2, 2016.

[162] Only a handful of other music videos from the 1990s even address environmental issues: Julian Lennon's "Saltwater" (1991), also directed by Nick Brandt, Kenny Loggins' "Conviction of the Heart (1991), and Vanessa Williams' "Colors of the Wind" (from the 1995 Disney film, Pocahontas). But none of these came close to the power and artistry of "Earth Song."

[163] *Keep Moving: The Michael Jackson Chronicles.* Resistance Works. 76-79.

[164] Michael Jackson's *This Is It.* DVD. Sony Pictures, 2010.

[165] "Black Ain't Green: Honoring Michael's Environmental Consciousness and Philanthropic Endeavors." Schomburg Center for Research in Black Culture. http://www.nypl.org/audiovideo/black-ain%E2%80%99t-green-honoring-michael%E2%80%99s-environmental-consciousness-and-philanthropic-endeav. June 5, 2010.

[166] Author Interview with Trisha Franklin. June 1, 2011. "Earth Song's" call-to-arms continues to inspire new generations. After seeing the *Earth Song* music video, one sensitive ten-year-old named Draven was so profoundly moved he pledged to tell everyone he knew about its message. He hadn't known about most of the issues the video portrayed and told his grandmother it "made him realize how important it is to take care of the earth." Author Interview with Mary House. June 4, 2011. The

parents of a three-year-old girl tell a similar story. One day they stumbled upon Jackson's video on YouTube. "[Our daughter] was profoundly moved," writes her mother, Danika Carter. "The first time I saw the video myself I was concerned that [my husband] was showing this to our then [three-year-old]...I was concerned that she was too young to see it, to understand its message and to see the pain and sadness. But I was wrong. This was the day my [daughter] became an environmentalist. She was so moved by the video that she kept asking me why the people were so sad, and why people hurt the animals and the earth. It was a wonderful opportunity to talk to her about how the decisions we make affect the environment, animals, and our community."
"Teaching Children To Honor the Earth." http://www.drgreene.com/perspectives/2011/03/16/teaching-children-honor-earth. March 16, 2011.
[167] Michael Jackson Fan Club. News Archives. June 1999.
[168] Author Interview with Brad Buxer. June 12, 2011. Buxer adds: "It's incredible what Michael did that night. Any lesser performer would have stopped. He was pretty shaken, but he refused to cut the performance short."
[169] "What More Can I Give." Karen Faye. *Karen Faye – A Life Intersected.* July 27, 2010. Jackson, it should be noted, was lip synching to a backing track for this particular performance. Still, the fact that he survived the fall and continued performing is quite remarkable.
[170] According to Brad Buxer, the fall might have been much worse if not for an alert tech who helped slow the velocity of the falling bridge by getting some resistance on the cables.

[171] "What More Can I Give," *Karen Faye – A Life Intersected*. July 27, 2010.
[172] "Star Goes Down in a Blaze of Fire as Prop Collapses," *Daily Record*. June 29, 1999.
[173] "What More Can I Give," *Karen Faye – A Life Intersected*. July 27, 2010.
[174] The 3D short featured a young girl (played by Jasmine Alveran) who falls asleep in a forest, only to wake up to a burned down wasteland. 3D glasses were made available do the audience and to viewers at home via retailer Target.
[175] This tribute was introduced by "We Are the World" co-writer Lionel Richie and sung by Smokey Robinson, Usher, Jennifer Hudson, Carrie Underwood and Celine Dion. After the performance, Jackson's three children accepted a "Lifetime Achievement Award" on behalf of their father. Said Grammy producer Ken Ehrlich of the choice to use "Earth Song" of all the hits in his catalog to pay tribute to Jackson: "This felt to us like it was really a way of representing him. It's like a tip of the hat. This song was so important to him." "Michael Was Complex: Ken Ehrlich Discusses the Grammys' 3-D Tribute to Jackson." Todd Martens. *Pop & Hiss* Music Blog. *The Los Angeles Times*. January 20, 2010.
[176] "Michael Jackson 'Earth Song' Tribute Focuses on His Love of the Planet." Shaheem Reid. MTV.com. http://www.mtv.com/news/articles/1630895/michael-jackson-grammy-tribute-focuses-on-his-love-planet.jhtml. January 31, 2010.
[177] Michael Jackson's *This Is It*. Directed by Kenny Ortega. DVD. Sony Pictures, 2009.
[178] *Ibid*.
[179] *Ibid*.

Printed in Poland
by Amazon Fulfillment
Poland Sp. z o.o., Wrocław